The Open Way

The Open Way

a Meditation Handbook

Gerald G. May

PAULIST PRESS
New York, N.Y./Ramsey, N.J.

Copyright ©1977 by Gerald G. May

Interior design by Nigel Rollings
Line illustrations by Richard Rossitter

Library of Congress Catalogue Card Number: 77-70641

ISBN: 0-8091-0228-5

Published by Paulist Press
Editorial Office: 1865 Broadway, New York, N.Y., 10023

Business Office: 545 Island Road, Ramsey, N.J., 07446

Printed and bound in the United States of America

Table of Contents

Part I: Foundations

Chapter 1   Toward An Ecology of Consciousness   1
Chapter 2   Awareness   9
Chapter 3   Trying to Be Who We Already Are   13
Chapter 4   Presence: The Basic Practice of   19
                 Informal Meditation
Chapter 5   Mini-Meditations   27
Chapter 6   Allowing Mind to Be: The Basic Practice
                 of Formal Meditation   31
Chapter 7   Mind and Me   37

Part II: Ground Rules For Formal Meditation

Chapter 8   Being Gentle   47
Chapter 9   Time   51
Chapter 10   Place   55
Chapter 11   Body   59
Chapter 12   Relaxing   69
Chapter 13   Breathing   75
Chapter 14   Handling "Distractions"   81
Chapter 15   Effort   87

Part III: Bases For Formal Meditation

Chapter 16   The Centering Process   95
Chapter 17   Choosing a Method   101
Chapter 18   With Breathing or Sound as Base   107
Chapter 19   With Visual Image as Base   115
Chapter 20   Words: Scripture, Koan and Prayer   121
Chapter 21   With Body as Base   125
Chapter 22   With Miscellaneous Senses as Base   129
Chapter 23   With Mind as Base   133
Chapter 24   The Simplest of Bases   141

Part IV: Appendix

A.   The Entrapment of Human Awareness   143
B.   The Price of Paying Attention   148
C.   Growth Into Spiritual Longing   154
D.   The Forms of Meditation   158
E.   The Myth of Meditative Passivity   164
F.   Questions to Ask Your "Self"   170
G.   Meditative Trouble Shooting   175

To
Christine Duda and Barry Hurwitz

A way is only *the* way
when one finds it
and follows it oneself.
—Carl Jung

Part I

Foundations

Chapter One

Toward an Ecology of Consciousness

"Let us a little permit Nature to take her own way; she better understands her own affairs than we."
Michel Eyquem de Montaigne
Essays, Book III, Ch. 13

How-to-books
I sit in a library surrounded by "how-to" books. How to do this. How to be that. I am struck that these books can be divided into three groups: the helpful, the meaningless and the obscene.

The helpful are those which give me information about something I want to do. How To Fertilize Your Lawn. Guitar Playing for People with Five Thumbs. The Klutz's Guide to Car Repair. The meaningless are those in which I simply find no interest. It's just a matter of taste. Might be very interesting to someone else. Ten Steps to Giant African Violets. Home Dentistry. A Layman's Guide to the Gross National Product.

But the obscene are a different matter. They do not simply suggest ways of doing something. They say that one should alter or fix the way one *is*. They go beyond ways of doing and suggest ways of being.

Since this book speaks of awareness and being, and since it suggests a host of things to do, it is entirely possible that it might be obscene. I would hope that it will not be suggesting that you change the way you are. I would hope that it might in the long run help you let yourself *be* who you are. Whether this becomes obscene or not will depend largely on your attitude; whether you can make it through all the words and ideas and suggestions without making a thing of yourself.

There is a very thin line between altering the ways one does things and trying to alter the way one is. It is a difficult line, and very dangerous.

Human beings have trouble letting anything be—especially themselves. Being the only creatures with fully functional hands, we seem especially proud of our hands. And it seems we want to get them all over everything within reach. Human beings are active creatures. They have great abilities to control themselves and the world around them. To fix things, change things, improve upon and alter things. This is our blessing and our curse, for we always seem to be going overboard with our power.

Intoxicated with technological and psychological abilities, human beings often go beyond the natural levels of control that are necessary for civilization, survival and art. They career onward in great sweeping attempts to master everything. To force nature into total submission to human will. To change the basic life processes of humanity so that people can be "happier." To alter the essential psyche, soul and spirit of human beings, so that people as well as things can somehow be "better." In this process of course, people become things too. And they begin to feel separate, artificial, unnatural. Even one's self becomes a kind of a thing. An object to be bettered. And it too becomes separate.

It is perhaps our "nature" to walk this fierce and delicate line between doing what needs to be done and doing more than what needs to be done. Certainly the great ecological mistakes of the past century bear this out. It seems somehow natural and necessary that people till the soil to provide food. But at some point, with the extra additions of too many chemicals, too many dammed up rivers, and too many corporate markets, it is obvious that we have gone too far. It seems natural that people use wood to build houses and fences, but at some point, when an entire forest area has been stripped clean, we know we have gone overboard. It seems natural that there be some industry to make tools and machines for our welfare, but at some point when those industries have ruined the rivers and poisoned the air, we know we have overstepped.

Ecology-Line Always one can look back and say: "At some point we went too far." But at what point? Where is that delicate place where being-naturally becomes transformed into being-manipulatively? Where growth decays into building, healing into fixing, being into striving? When did we stop being a part of nature and start feeling apart *from* nature?

There is no rational, objective map which can be used to locate the point of going too far. But if one's eyes were open, perhaps one could see a change in feeling, a subtle alteration of attitude and awareness which takes place when one reaches that point. When one is tilling the soil, felling trees or working a machine, one begins with a feeling of being a part of a process. One feels a deep relationship, perhaps even a unity with what one is doing. In tilling the soil, the farmer may feel as if he were very much like the rains and the winds. His hands and the soil are like brother and sister. Felling a tree, there is the possibility of sensing the great process of growth and death of living things. The woodsman may even speak to the tree: "I cut you down now, tree, for a house or a fence. But I know you have lived as I have lived. And I know that sometime I shall be cut down too. We are together here, in this."

Working a machine, the laborer may sense the harmony of metal parts, the dance of his hands and the machine and the product, a symphony of motion. An appreciation of the process.

It seems to me that these feelings, these attitudes are the mark of naturalness. Of human beings being as they were meant to be—a part of the awesome process of this universe. When the decay starts, when the natural becomes artificial, when being becomes lost in power, there is a change in these feelings. The sense of distance between us and the soil or the tree or the machine becomes greater. In the process of decay, oneness becomes relationship, and relationship turns into

separateness, and the separateness into thingness and
alienation. We become strangers to our surroundings, and
our surroundings become objects. Their life, their rhythm,
their dance are gone. From there on out we begin to feel
contrived, and it is obvious that we have gone too far. Is it
possible then that the line between doing and overdoing is
not so much determined by our actions as by our inner state
of mind? If so, and if our eyes are open, perhaps we could
know it, immediately, when we start to cross that line. Let
me share two stories which bear on this.

The Carpenter
Not long ago I decided to build a bookcase. I chose the
lumber carefully, running my hands over the grain of the
wood, sensing its softness. I remember smelling the
fragrance of its cut edges. I brought it home, laid out the
tools and began to work. For a while I sensed the movements
of my hands and the tools, seeing form take shape as I
worked, appreciating.

Then something didn't fit quite right. I'd cut a piece of
wood just a fraction of an inch too long, and things changed.
Gradually I stopped being aware of the process of the work
and became more concerned with building the bookcase
right. Will it come out straight? Will it look good? Will it
hold together? Then the bookcase had become a *thing*,
which I was going to *make*. In my mind, all I could see was a
sort of worried picture of the thing already done. And I
began to wonder how long it would take. To wish it were
finished. This beautiful process, of which I had been so
much a part, now I was wishing it were finished. At that
point my awareness of the immediate process had been
killed. I was up somewhere in the future, worrying about the
product, the *outcome*.

I cut the piece of wood again. This time it was too short.
Frustration. Pound the sides in to make it fit. Hammer marks
in the wood. Anger. Wishing it were finished. Force it
together. Make it fit. Looks rough. I had wanted the grain to
show, but now I'll have to paint it to cover up the
roughness. What do I have to do at work next week? Oh, I
wish this were finished.

It got finished. And it didn't look too bad. It sits in our
living room. I made it. But walking by it, seeing it there, I am
sometimes tempted to ask, "What happened to us,
bookcase? You and I were together for a while. And now
you are a thing."

The point of decay is not so hard to see. It happened
when my awareness got trapped. When it got hijacked away
from the immediate moment. That was the clue. That's when
it happened.

The Bug
One winter when I was about ten, I found a small
brown cocoon-type object and brought it into the house. I
didn't know what it was until several weeks later, when I
came home from school and found hundreds of little praying
mantises all over the house. There was a problem of what to
do with them. The warmth had caused them to hatch
prematurely, and I couldn't release them into the still-possi-
ble freezes of the outside. So I set about to feed them. I

prepared aphids, mites, even tiny pieces of hamburger for their dinners. But most of the time they ate each other. Repeatedly. Their numbers thus decreasing consistently, those who remained appeared quite healthy.

They went, as I remember it, through two or three molts, shedding their old skins and doubling in size each time. The molting seemed very difficult for them. A bit like delivering oneself in childbirth. Many of them died in the process of molting, stuck halfway out of their old skins, helpless prey for their marauding brothers and sisters. Finally the ravages of man-made diet, artificial warmth, cannibalism and self-birth took their toll, and only one was left. I remember him very clearly, a beautiful brown-green color, eyes bright. He was perhaps an inch long as the time for his next molt approached. He had become rather special to me because he was the only survivor. We had something of a relationship.

But then he began to molt, and he got stuck. Or appeared to. He struggled for fifteen minutes, halfway out of his old outside, without any apparent progress. He looked tired. I tried to help him. I moistened his old skin with water, hoping to soften it a bit. But he remained stuck. And I began to feel frustrated. I really wanted him to live, and I wasn't having any effect on his struggle. That's when the point came. Being with him in his growth had ceased for me. Now he was a thing I wanted to have. It was at that precise point that awareness became stifled by my desire to have what I wanted. It was as if I had slipped into a robotic, programmed, automatic pilot, wanting to achieve my objective. I got a pair of tweezers and tried, ever so gently, to pry him out. And he broke in half.

I remember struggling then with the question: At what point had I gone too far? Should I have just let him struggle? Or waited longer? Would he really have died anyway? When should I have stopped trying to "help"?

Those questions, crude and poorly formed in the mind of a ten year old boy, were about a bug. Now I ask those questions about a lot of things. Knowing that one can be actively involved in the processes of living, healing, growing; knowing that one *must* be involved in these processes, one wonders repeatedly how to know when one has gone too far.

Now, in retrospect, I think I have a clue. It is not so much in what one does as in what happens to awareness. It is when awareness gets killed. When the programs of power, accomplishment, manipulation and achievement take over. When our beautiful hands, dancing with the world, become grubby hands messing with it. That's when we go too far.

Alteration of consciousness The examples I have given have to do with real "things," fields and trees, machines, bookcases and bugs. But the "thing" I'm most concerned about here is not a thing at all. It is the way we approach our minds, our being, our spirit, our awareness. With the myriad of psychotherapeutic, human growth and consciousness-alteration techniques presented to western civilization during the past century, it is obvious that we have come to deal with our "selves" in much the same way as I dealt with the bookcase and the bug. The sense of self has become a thing to be improved upon. And in the process one comes to feel separate from "it." The mind has become a thing to be fixed, repaired and controlled. And consciousness, the very essence of appreciation of being, has become a thing to be "altered." Altered states of consciousness. Consciousness raising. Consciousness expansion. Awareness training.

Make no mistake about it. We are attempting to do "to" consciousness what we have done "to" the rivers and the forests. It may be in pursuit of wholeness, peace or even naturalness that we seek to alter consciousness, but when that line is crossed and awareness becomes a thing to be done unto, wholeness, peace and naturalness may as well be forgotten. In fact by that time they *have* been forgotten.

The alteration of consciousness is to me one of the most obscene phrases of our time. It reminds me of how one alters animals to make eunuchs of them. And it tempts me to ask the timeworn question: "Is nothing sacred?"

If it seems I make too much of this, it is because I am aware of my own treacherous tendencies to want to alter my being and the being of those around me. And it is because I know how terribly seductive these tendencies can be. And finally it is because this book has much to do with awareness, waking up, opening eyes, freely being now. Even though it will be said time and again that the only hope for freely being and for freedom for awareness is to let oneself be, I know how easy it will be to make an object of awareness. Something more to be managed. And there is great danger in this. In working with your hands, your awareness can inform you when you start to go too far. But if you start to alter your own consciousness, and it too becomes a thing, what is left to tell you where you are?

Freeing awareness Sensing that awareness-trapping is what robs one of being in the process of life, one wants to learn how to help awareness be more free. Free and present here and now without so much management. To be on automatic pilot less of the time and wide-awake more of the time. This is precisely the theme of this book, and at the same time its greatest danger. In trying to loosen the cords with which awareness is bound, will we wind up binding it even further?

This book is full of exercises, experiences, things to do. It is my hope that these ideas and suggestions will have an overall effect of easing the bonds of awareness, and of allowing one to be fully and freely who one is. But that is a very treacherous hope, and one would perhaps do well to be without it altogether. To forget it. If that were only possible. To move into the process of these experiences *for no reason at all.* Because the reason is very likely to invade the process, and the result will then be precisely what happened to my bug.

Accepting It would feel safe, even comfortable if we could indeed forget our reasons, stifle our expectations and kill our hopes for accomplishment. But this would also be to kill who we are, and thank God that is not ultimately possible. We are then committed, whether we like it or not, to walk the dangerous line. To be uncomfortable with it. To face the fires of our own treachery. To feel the airy pain of the peeling-off of layers of management and manipulation, and the heavy pain of adding different, more subtle layers of management and manipulation. To stomach our repeated mistakes and somehow try to accept them.

In the process of "trying" to allow awareness to fly free, to let ourselves be, we will be tempted to dull that very awareness, to close our eyes through not wishing to see our failure and through becoming fixated on our desires and expectations. One can only do one's best, and that means repeated failure. The most painful thing of all will be to keep one's eyes open in the midst of this, *and not ultimately try to do anything at all to fix it.*

Chapter Two

Awareness

"To be awake is to be alive."
Henry David Thoreau,
Walden

Losing awareness
For most people, most of the time, awareness is trapped. Try an exercise right now. Take a few minutes and become aware of being here, reading. Remain in this simple, open state and see what happens. Watch carefully until you realize you've "lost" it.

Then try another experiment. Concentrate very closely on the period at the end of this paragraph. When it seems very clear to you, close your eyes and be aware of what's happening in your mind.

Immediately after your eyelids met, there was a brief instant of totally quiet awareness. Free of thought, image, sensation. Immediate and open. Then some mental activity began. It may have been a visual image, a recognition of darkness or quiet, or some other sensation. Then there probably were some thoughts. Perhaps, "Here I am" or "What should I expect?" or "Is this what I'm supposed to be doing?" or something. Some kind of labeling or judging of the experience. And at some point in all of this, awareness began to get trapped. You "lost" it. See if you can remember when and how that happened. Try it again if you wish, and watch, carefully. Don't try to hold on to awareness. Just watch to see when and where it "goes."

How much of the time is awareness "gone" like that? For most people, a lot. And one senses it would be sort of nice to have awareness "back." To be wide awake, here, now, realizing one is living, appreciating the process of being. Even more, to become one with living, fully immersed in life with eyes wide open.

Avoiding pain
Why is it that we aren't awake more of the time? What happens to pull us "out" of life, to make us feel separate and distanced? For one thing, we don't like pain very much. And life is often painful. The tendency is to block out awareness of life in order to avoid the pain it may hold. Like taking a narcotic. As if it were better to be unaware than to be aware of something unpleasant. This pattern causes people to want to cheat a bit on life. "I'll have the pleasure, without the pain, please." But of course that's really impossible. Pleasure doesn't even mean anything except in relationship to pain. It's impossible to have one without the other, no matter how hard one may try.

So we may tend to kill the whole business. "I'm going to sleep now. Wake me up when things are more fun." It's like the experience most of us have had with young love. At the end of one's first love, the pain is so great that one often resolves never to fall in love again. "I'll do without the pleasure, because the pain is just too much. I don't want to be hurt anymore." So one tries to do without love. The same thing happens with awareness.

Management and control

Another reason, and I think a more important reason why we kill awareness is that we are born managers. Human beings feel that they must somehow manage every single thing that enters their awareness. In some way, everything must be *dealt* with. Every sensation, every thought, everything must have something made of it. It must be used, modified, integrated, manipulated, understood, interpreted, evaluated, controlled. At the very least, it must be labeled. Got to get our hands on it somehow.

It has been so ingrained in us to be in control of ourselves (whatever our "selves" are) that every experience becomes an object to be taken charge of. Of course this takes an incredible amount of energy. And of course it's very crazy indeed. If one really *were* consciously in charge of everything, one would be paralyzed. One could not even lift a finger. The complex sequence of intent, nerve conduction, muscle contraction, sensory feedback and such required to lift a finger is simply too much to handle. For anyone. But that doesn't keep us from trying.

A good example of this, and one that's readily available, is breathing. All along, you're breathing. But are *you* doing it? When you're not aware of it are you doing the breathing any more than you're doing the beating of your heart? When you're not paying attention to your breathing, it runs along fine.

But right now, try paying attention to your breathing. Just sit still for one or two minutes and watch your breathing. See if you can do that without messing with your breath. See if it is possible for you to *allow* your breathing to be natural. Most people can't—not without practice. For most people, awareness is so glued to the idea of control that one just seems to accompany the other wherever they go.

Sit sometime outside in the breeze. There is incredible beauty in sensing the breeze upon your face and never once calling it "breeze." This is something that all of us have experienced, long ago, when we were very young. But it is a beauty forgotten.

With the attitude that anything coming into consciousness must somehow be dealt with, it seems like being awake takes a lot of work. So in order to ease off the work a little, we tend to keep ourselves asleep a good deal of the time. And, when there is some special task to be accomplished, we tend to stifle our awareness of everything else. We call this "paying attention," and we are seldom aware of how much additional effort we have to put into blocking out everything *except* the object of our attention. We arbitrarily define what is important to be aware of and what is not. We select one thing to focus on and label all the rest as "distractions." Then we work very hard to shut out the "distractions" and concentrate on the task. And afterwards, we find ourselves tired. But it wasn't just the work on the task that created fatigue. It was all the effort that went into shutting everything else out.

No wonder then that one comes home from the office and grabs a martini, or that one collapses into a chair and turns on the TV when the kids are finally off to school. No wonder "taking it easy" usually means to block *everything* out. So there's nothing needing to be managed. And it's no wonder that this kind of taking it easy often makes us more tired than ever.

Fear of death Finally, there is another explanation for why people like to spend so much time unaware. This is the most important reason of all, and in one way or another it underlies and determines all the rest. It is the fear of death.

Just being When awareness is free, and when one is deeply, openly immersed in the process of living, one is not in the business of defining oneself. If one is in a state of unity with life and the world, one cannot ask, "Who am I?" As long as awareness is truly free and one is "just" being, one cannot be concerned with self-importance or self-degradation. Identity is meaningless. And when we cease to define ourselves, we become frightened. It is something like death. Non-existence.

Defining self Ironically, it is in those moments when one is most fully freely living that one tends to pull back, suddenly realizing that the self has been forgotten, afraid of continuing to be. For it is not in being, but in *trying* to be, that one defines one's self. It is in the doing, the achievement, the relationships, the control, mastery and manipulation that one carves out identity. It is in making marks upon the world, upon oneself, and upon others that one creates an image of "who I am." How precious this identity seems to us, that we would sacrifice our very awareness of being in order to cling to it.

This is a very ancient problem, faced in one way or another by every person since the time human beings created words. As soon as people started to label the "things" around them, they started to label themselves. And ever since, the great "I AM" has captured awareness for all humankind.

World religions The major religions of the world have offered ways out of this trap. They all begin with some core statement to the effect, "I AM THAT I AM." How can *that* be managed? How is anyone going to meddle with *that*? And they all carry the message that one doesn't *have* to meddle with it. Christianity, Buddhism, Islam, Judaism, Hinduism, all proclaim in their various ways a deep reassurance that it is in losing one's self that one finds oneself. That it is in dying that one finds life. All promise that if one could but give up the struggle for self-definition, being would spring forth in fullness and truth.

But the promise is a hard one. It seems the sacrifice is too great. People remain enmeshed in their struggle to master living. And awareness remains trapped.

Chapter Three

Trying To Be
Who We Already Are

"It is an honor for a man to cease from strife; but every fool
will be meddling."
Proverbs 20:3

Experiencing being

It might be comfortable, or at least tolerable, to remain
in the trap of management, self-definition and stifled
awareness, if it were not for one thing. The problem is that
we are treated, now and then, to moments of spontaneously
free awareness. This is both a curse and blessing. The curse
is that free awareness never seems to last for long. Just long
enough to tantalize us with a glimpse of freely being, just as
we are. Only long enough to create a dissatisfaction with our
habitual working-at-life. The blessing, of course, is that we
are privileged to experience such moments at all.

I remember a fall evening when I was in college. I was
walking back to my dormitory after several hours of
studying for an exam. My mind was in that special tired-yet-
invigorated state that comes after a piece of unusually hard
work has been completed. It was as if my mind were taking a
break from thinking.

As I crossed a small grassy knoll I suddenly stopped,
caught up by the night. I stood very still, and in that
moment I was at one with the grass, the warm autumn wind,
the stars. I stood there as if I'd grown there, just like the
trees. There was incredible vastness and simplicity. All
seemed to be just as it should be. There was no yesterday, no
tomorrow, no this or that, no me or it. No labels at all, not
even of myself. Yet everything was there, vibrant, open, and
exquisitely beautiful.

I have no idea how long it lasted, but I do remember
how it ended. It ended when somewhere deep inside, my
image of myself had been threatened enough and began to
reassert power. The thought came, "My God, how beautiful
this is." And with that, I began to meddle. To label and
evaluate the experience, and to define myself. Even in the
guise of wanting the experience to continue, I was back in
the business of management and meddling. And with that
the experience ceased. Everything went back to "normal."
But I was left with a certitude that normal wasn't really
normal anymore. Things had turned around. That
experience, which had seemed so special and out of the
ordinary, was in fact a simple, clear perception of the way I
really am. And my usual habitual perception of myself as a
separate "thing" was grossly mistaken.

It is tempting to make a big deal out of this kind of
experience. Call it peak, or mystical, transcendent, cosmic,
the Peace that passeth all understanding, union with God.
"It" has been a big deal for millennia. Every major religion,

every great literary endeavor, every lasting work of art has somehow alluded to "it." Ever since mankind's words created the wound of separation between self and other, people have made a big deal out of being at one again. But to make it so special is really rather ironic. For "it" is just naturally the way we really are. We're simply so busy defining ourselves away from our true nature that when our eyes clear and we *see*, it does indeed seem like something special.

Even the seeing is not all that out of the ordinary. People are having experiences like this all the time. Often the experiences are so quickly squelched by the reassertion of self-image that they are hardly noticed. Even the experiences which are noticed are often quickly forgotten. Or repressed. Because of their great threat. For in spite of the beauty of oneness, unity and self-definition cannot co-exist. When one is seen, the other dies. So we often "forget" those brief instants of clearly seeing the way we really are. But nearly everyone, with but a little effort at recollection, can remember many times when the clear vision of truth just seemed to happen.

Perhaps it is because people spend so much of their time in self-defining activities, because they are so *used* to feeling separate, that experiences of unity seem like something to be achieved. To be sought after. Perhaps this is why we so often feel we must do something extra or travel somewhere else in order to arrive at where we really are right now. Or perhaps it is because we never learned that there might be value in relaxing instead of struggling, or in not-doing instead of doing.

Trying to   For whatever reason, it is likely that we will try to "get" the experiences, to go chasing after them through prayer or meditation or deep relationships or psychedelic drugs or self-realization. Trying to collect as many peak experiences as possible. Wanting to achieve an endless one. That was what I did for a while. Then I became more "sophisticated" and started thinking that to collect peak experiences was of little real value. The experiences had to be "integrated" with the whole of one's ongoing life. That sounds better, perhaps, but it is still absolutely crazy. It's funny enough to think of people trying to chase after and achieve the way they really are. But it's almost hilarious when I watch myself trying to "integrate" the way I really am with the way I think I am. At least it's a fun thing to do on a Saturday afternoon.

In actuality, I suppose the only means of being who you are is simply to relax and be who you are. You can't manufacture reality. You can't achieve natural being. You can't create truth. One can only hope that by relaxing and allowing oneself to be, one will begin to see and appreciate how one really is.

But we are bound to try to do more about it. That's simply another part of the way we really are. If it is understood that natural being can be perceived only when awareness is free of management and self-definition, then we are likely to try to stop managing and to cease defining ourselves. But that's a willful impossibility. It throws one into a morass of paradox.

If I try to cease managing, is that not another management? If I try to quit defining myself, am I not still there saying: "Here I am stopping my self-definition"? Or perhaps I shall try to lose myself in order to find my true nature. But that will be very difficult indeed. It is not easy to lose something intentionally. One always seems to remember where one left it. Even if I try to offer myself to God, I will still be standing there, holding out my hands, the one who is doing the giving. If I say and truly mean "Thy will be done," I'm still the one saying it, wishing it. And even if out of the despair of this I try to kill my image of myself, there I am again, the murderer.

So what does one do?

There are several options which are not terribly crazy.

Sane possibilities One is to accept one's predicament, hope and pray that salvation or redemption or enlightenment or release will occur, and then simply go about living the best way one can. Perhaps trusting in Grace or the Will of God or the Unfolding Process of the Cosmos to extricate us when the time is right.

Or one can accept the predicament and simply acknowledge that it is mankind's destiny, for whatever metaphysical reason, to be caught in a delusion. And to know it is a delusion. And yet to be unable to get out of it.

Or one can accept the predicament *and* accept one's own attempts to get out of it, and hope and pray for the best. Recognizing the trap, and recognizing our desire to do something to get out of the trap, and recognizing the paradoxical humor of our attempts, we go ahead and try.

Humor, it seems, is absolutely necessary. For sanity and energy. Here we are, struggling to find a way to become what we already are. And here is this book, offering a host of "techniques" to help us be who we already are. This kind of craziness can either be dreadfully painful or terrifically funny. It might as well be funny.

One's attitude then could be to accept one's own craziness, and to accept one's own crazy attempts to get out of the craziness, and then go ahead and work like blazes just to be. Keeping all the while a small grin.

Then through all the techniques, all the doings, all the trying-to-be, the theme will be to allow oneself to return to one's own natural state of being. Not to make it or achieve it but to allow it to happen. To allow the delusion and the management and the meddling and the self-definition to pass away, as it will, when it will, until the clear open wordless truth of the way-it-really-is can be seen.

It's like letting a pendulum come to rest, or a turbulent pool of water settle into quietude. The work of it is to keep our grubby hands off. It is not possible to use your fingers to set a pendulum in its natural center point. It will never be quite right. Ultimately, it must come to rest by itself. You

can perhaps slow it a little around the edges, keep it from too
great extremes, but in the last analysis it must find its own
center.

The same is true of waves on the water. You can't press
them into stillness. You might, perhaps, try to keep
additional stresses from creating *more* waves, but at the end
of it all, you must allow the water to become still by itself.
That's the way it is with your being, or your "self," or your
awareness. Or your mind. It is possible to do some things
around the edges, to simplify the noisy busy-ness of it all,
but the final doing must be not-doing. You must, finally,
sometime, let yourself be. Which is a bit of a relief, because
you are who you are anyway, no matter what you do.

In the doing, then, it is important not to try to add too
much to yourself, nor to subtract anything in excess. Not to
achieve too much, nor to negate too much. But to dance with
gentleness around the edges of your management and self-
definition.

It may help to nurture an attitude of pretending.
Whatever you do to try to be, it's sort of like pretending to
be. You are a pretender to the throne of being. Your practice
then is not like that of athletics or music. There really is
nothing to be achieved.

Meditation Most of the practices suggested in this book are
endeavors to allow oneself to be. Letting mind, body,
consciousness just be as they are for a while. Not to alter
consciousness. Not to impose anything. Especially not to try
to impose naturalness. But to allow ourselves to settle down
into the naturalness which is already there. To get our
grubby hands off ourselves without killing awareness in the
process.

These kinds of practices are called meditation. There are
many kinds of meditation, and meditation can be "used" for
many different purposes.[1] But it is best not to worry too
much about one's objective. Let us lightly accept that
meditation is simply something to do when we feel it is
necessary to do something about being. That's all.

I've spent quite a long time trying to figure out what
meditation is. Happily, I have not been very successful. But
for what it may be worth, I'll share a list of definitions I've
used. They are all both "correct" and grossly inadequate.
And they stand as evidence of the complexity one
encounters in trying to figure it out, even when one attempts
to keep things as simple as possible. Meditation is:

1. Non-judgmental alertness
2. Relaxed attentiveness
3. Allowing what is
4. Making friends with your mind
5. Being aware of awareness
6. Being aware of being
7. Just being aware
8. Waking up. Now! Snap your fingers, slap your
face. Thanks, I needed that.
9. Relaxing with bright, sharp, clear awareness

with no effort whatsoever

11. Doing what comes naturally

12. Simply being aware of who you are, where you are, right now

13. The listening half of prayer

14. The space after a sigh

15. Letting the mind go back, like a relaxing muscle, to its natural state. And going with it. Letting it be what it is. Whatever it is.

16. No expectations, no trying, no effort

17. No trying not to try

18. Keeping your grubby hands off yourself without sitting on your hands

19. Pretending to be trying to be who you already are

20. Just being

There are three ways of understanding something. The first is to think and talk about it. This is very complex. The second is to do something with it. This is, hopefully, more simple. The third is to be it. This is so incredibly simple that our complexity-habituated minds can seldom cope with it. There must be a balance between these three, and there has now been enough talking. It is time to move into doing. The being will come, as it will come.

1. See Appendix

Chapter Four

The Basic Practice of Informal Meditation

"It is eternity now. I am in the midst of it. It is about me in the sunshine; I am in it, as the butterfly in the light-laden air. Nothing has to come; it is now. Now is eternity; now is the immortal life."

Richard Jefferies,
The Story of My Heart

Two styles   There are two basic styles in meditation. One is *formal* meditation, in which you set aside some special time and place to be alone with your mind when there's not too much else going on. The other style is *informal* meditation, which occurs all during the rest of your day, and consists of just watching, seeing everything. It is a very simple matter of gently becoming aware, immediately, here and now. So give yourself a little time set aside each day to be with your mind, and the rest of the time—just watch.

Formal meditation, with its exotic and mystical connotations, is perhaps more colorful and enticing than the simple presence of informal meditation. But it is informal meditation that comes closer to just being. Because it takes place within the very course of natural living, informal meditation is really a much purer practice. If meditation is a practice of pretending to let yourself be who you already are, then formal meditation is a practice for informal meditation, and informal meditation a practice for spontaneous meditation, and spontaneous meditation a practice for just being.

There are many people who feel they need to do something to wake up to their natural being, yet cannot seem to sit still for formal meditation. They get bored or anxious or fed up with the craziness of it, and they just simply can't "do" it. It may well be that for them formal meditation is as unnecessary as it is impossible. But for anyone, every act of living can be meditation. Every movement can be prayer. Every breath and event can be the gentle nudge which wakes us up.

A gentle nudge is all it takes. The force of a falling snowflake to bring yourself into immediate awareness whenever it occurs to you. You "do" this in the midst of whatever happens to be going on at the time. In the middle of a business meeting or bathing the kids or arguing with your boss or digging in your garden or taking a shower or eating lunch or driving your car or going to school or going to the bathroom or reading the paper or *whatever*, you just nudge yourself into awareness. Just for a moment.

Buddhism has a story of Buddha meeting a woman at a well. His words to her were, "Watch your hands as you draw the water." That's all there is to it.

1. PERCEPTION

Try adopting the attitude of watching all the things you're involved with as if they were clouds in the sky. As if you were lying on a hillside, watching them go by. Another way is to see it all, *all* of life as if it were a dream. Or simply take a deep breath, let it clear your eyes, and see what is.

2. DOING THINGS DIFFERENTLY

Pick out something you habitually do, and change it. Do it differently. For example, if you usually wear a ring on one finger, switch it to another. Dumb little things like that. The dumber the better. If you normaly slouch when you sit, try sitting up straight. Or vice versa. If you usually walk with your toes out or in, walk with them straight ahead. Or become aware of your center of gravity, a couple of inches beneath your navel, and let all your movements come from there instead of from your head. Look at yourself and pick out some nondescript habit and change it just a little. This will help bring you into awareness more often as you go through the day.

3. KEEPING SOMETHING IN YOUR HEART

Pick some silent mantra, prayer, sound or image, plant it deep inside you, and let it go on by itself. You don't have to say it or work at it. Just plant it and let it go. Then, in little moments of pause throughout the day, you can listen to it. Take a little care in selecting this. Be sure it's something you're willing to have go deep down inside you and stay there.

4. WORKING WITH DESIRE

Take something you like doing and do just a little less of it. Just a little. Not so you're really hurting, but just to be a bit short of total satisfaction. Just the edge. Eat a little less, smoke a little less, sleep a little less, work a little less, talk a little less. Something light and not very important. And keep it light. This is not an exercise in asceticism, nor is it something you should do in order to break a habit. If it starts getting heavy or serious, watch out. Martyrdom, masochism, extreme austerity and self-sacrifice can be very seductive awareness-trappers. They are much more sneaky than laziness, lethargy and sloth.

5. "GETTING INTO NOW"

The immediate moment

Probably the simplest and often the best way to nurture the presence of informal meditation is to move very directly into awareness of the immediate moment. Even when there's a lot of stress going on and your attention is repeatedly getting lost, just tune in to whatever is happening right now. If you need to, you can whisper "Now" to yourself, and then simply see.

Opening within and without

Don't feel you have to label or judge anything, stifle or turn away from anything. Just open to what's going on around and within you. This includes all the sights, sounds, colors, textures, forms and activities in the world immediately around you. And it includes all the perceptions and feelings from your body. And it also includes whatever

 you sense is going on in your mind. Even if your mind is
thinking about the future, it is doing that now, and you can
see. Even if you are having some kind of memory, you're

Realizing "Getting into now" requires no change whatsoever in

 moment. You don't need to do anything to "get" there. All
you need is a little nudge into realizing it.

aying words Sometimes it is necessary to say some words to yourself
need to say: "Here I am, walking, with my hair blowing in
watching for cars." It may take this many words to help you
be aware at the beginning. But soon you can simplify it, and
you should. Pretty soon it can be, "Here I am, crossing the

Just sensing street." And then, "Crossing the street." Then all the words
can stop and you will be able just to sense. And there doesn't
need to be any labeling of it or thinking about it. Then your
toward this simplicity as soon as you can, so that you add no
Say the words to yourself only if it is impossible just
say no more than necessary. When you say the words, what
you are doing is sneaking up on the moment from behind.
Trying to outwit your self-identification which is always

-When you say aloud "Here I am, doing this," you're
 about one second behind the moment you were talking
 about.
 -When you say it silently, you're about ¾ of a second
 behind it.
 -When you drop the words "doing this," you're half a
 second away.
 -When you drop the "Here" and just think "I am,"
 about a quarter of a second.
 -When you drop the "I" it's only about a tenth of a
 second behind the moment.
 -Finally, when you drop the "am" and just sense, there
 you are. Or now you are. Where you were all along,
 only now your eyes are open.
See how complicated things can become when one
works at it? Always the thing to remember is to accept your
own need for complexity, but not to overdo it. Keep things as

Passive While you are sensing what's going on in the immediate
watching moment, the watching must be very passive. This doesn't
mean that *you* have to be passive. Just the watching.

That's not as easy as it may sound. Almost always at first the watching will include meddling. Just as it does when you become aware of your breathing. It's as if the watching becomes a separate kind of observer which starts mumbling things like, "Here I am, doing this. How *well* am I doing this? Maybe I could have done that better. Maybe I shouldn't *be* doing this. What shall I do next?" Or, "My, isn't this nice and quiet and beautiful!" Or, "This awareness-freeing business is really great." Or, "That's an airplane I hear." When the observer starts making noises like this, it means it's been caught up in meddling, and probably awareness has been caught too.

Avoiding meddling

When this happens, and it will, repeatedly, you can do one of three things. Relax and forget the whole business. Or relax and see if the observer won't shut up. Or relax and get another observer going to quietly watch the first observer making all the noise. Again, this can get very complicated, but the important thing is that when the observer gets noisy, that's the time to relax.

Remaining quiet

It takes a lot of gentleness, relaxation and acceptance for the watching to remain quiet. Acceptance must be as complete as is possible. However you find yourself, no matter *how* you find yourself, accept. For example, let's say you're angry with someone. Your habitual sequence of response will be something like the following:

1. Experience anger
2. Want to lash out
3. Common sense or conscience says "No"
4. Feel frustrated
5. Do something with the anger; express, repress, channel, etc.

Most of this sequence takes place unconsciously. It all just happens, like your breathing, while awareness is foggy or shut down entirely.

If you happen to become immediately aware at some point during this sequence, you will immediately try to get in there and manage it, make it more efficient, get the whole thing under control somehow. Soon it will become unclear as to what is happening as a result of your natural habits and what is due to your conscious engineering. All of this is fine, except that getting into the engineering will probably trap awareness, and you won't know when to stop meddling. You'll cross that ecology-line and things will get goofed up.

Being awake

Informal meditation means to encourage staying awake at a time like this. Or at any time. But without that increased awareness bringing further meddling along with it. You wake up not so that you can engineer things better, but simply so that you can see. And in the seeing itself will happen all the improvement or growth or healing that is necessary. If you become aware at any point in the anger sequence, all you need do is *accept* what's going on. Don't try to stop anything, or to speed anything up. Don't even try *not* to stop anything, or *not* to speed anything up. Just let it be as it is happening.

If you are able to keep the watching passive, you may

Just feeling find that you'll see the entire sequence of response to anger, and at the end of it you may feel that the situation is not fully resolved. You may still feel angry. That's because you're watching. When normally you would have repressed that left-over anger, now your eyes are open and you're just hanging out there with it, and there doesn't seem to be much more that you can do with it. At that point you may sense that you feel angry, but that to do anything more would surely stifle your awareness. That's beautiful. That's just the way it should be. Because you're at the ecology line—when doing anything more would be doing too much. At this point you may simply have to be angry. Sacrifice the modern psychological myth which says that all feeling must totally be taken care of. Accept the sanity of just having the feeling and not doing anything *about* it. Just simply to feel angry. Or scared, or sad, or anything. Just to feel it.

Seeing what is When you sense that doing something more will trap awareness, that is the time to stop and just have the feeling. Watch it. Move into it, go with it, sense it fully, be in it. Maybe, if you're open enough, you will even have the opportunity of following that feeling as it reverts into the raw, beautiful energy from whence it came. Again this is becoming complicated. Just remember that being awake right now really involves nothing more than seeing. Relaxing and opening to what is.

Nobody watching Another problem with this watching business is that you may begin to identify yourself with the one who's doing the watching. If you do, you'll begin to feel sort of "out of it," detached, distanced from life. If for example you are watching yourself pulling weeds, it may seem as if your identity, your center of being, your "self" is what is doing the watching. But that's not true. There is *nobody* watching. Watching is happening. If you're pulling weeds and watching, it's not somebody else pulling weeds while you watch. Nor is it somebody else watching while you're pulling weeds. It's best not to get hung up in this problem at all, but again simplicity is not always forthcoming. If you do start wondering "Am I doing, or watching, or both, or neither?" you can approach it from several ways.

Letting be You can understand that part of your mind is doing, and part is watching, and they're both you. And that at the same time you are a lot of other things; a body with weight and form, senses perceiving, lungs breathing, heart beating, energy dancing, all sorts of things. In the field of your consciousness, all these phenomena just appear like sparkles in the night and they can *all* be you. Or you can understand that in the midst of all this energetic activity, the whole idea of "you" is just another sparkle in the night. A label, another label, you've given to a certain collection of stuff. It really doesn't matter, as long as you don't use "It's all me" to feel big and important, and as long as you don't use "I am just a figment" to feel importantly meaningless. What does matter is not to cling too hard to any frozen image of who you are. Let it wax and wane as it will. Let it come and go. If that sense of a separate observer doing the watching does come up, and you begin to identify with it, just relax. Ideally, with enough gentleness and relaxation, that observer won't happen at all. But that ideal is something we simply have to wait for.

Relaxing   Most of all, you won't need to do anything to become aware during the process of your daily life. Most of all, you can simply relax and let yourself wake up, anytime, anywhere. Relaxing is probably the most basic element in waking up. It doesn't work to try to hold awareness tensely, or to struggle to stay awake. But the exact opposite, relaxing body and mind in the midst of everything, just lets waking up happen.

Mini-Meditations

"They surfeited with honey and began to loathe the taste of sweetness, whereof a little more than a little is by much too much."
William Shakespeare,
Henry IV, Part I

Between formal and informal   This is a little group of little meditations which form a transition between informal and formal practice. They are very short, and can happen almost anywhere and anytime. They're light and fun and simple, and can make a real difference in the middle of a busy day. But don't use them to get away from a busy day. Use them to get into it as it really is. They are simply little gimmicks to help wake up. Small breaths of air for a suffocating awareness. Nothing special.

The list given here is just for example. Come up with your own.

1. Light a match. Watch the flame. Just look at it as it burns. Then slowly blow it out and savor your awareness.

2. When you hear some music, let your breathing go with it for a while.

3. Look at your breathing. Just that. No interference. Simply watch. After you've been breathing for a while, stop for a few seconds, in between breaths. Hear the silence.

4. Look at a spot on the wall for a few seconds. Then close your eyes. See the emptiness.

5. Memorize a little child's prayer or song. In the midst of something very adult and important, recite it gently to yourself.

6. Sit very still. See your body quiet and solid, like a mountain.

7. If a breeze blows past you, stop for a moment and feel it.

8. As you walk, breathe in time to your steps.

9. Sit with your eyes closed. Begin counting slowly, silently in your mind. Picture the numbers; imagine what they look like as you count. Then stop! Immediately, be aware of the absolute stillness.

10. As you're driving, sense your hands holding the wheel, your body responding to the traffic.

11. When you pull in to park and turn off the engine, listen to the silence. Or when you turn off the TV or the shower. When any sound stops, just listen to what's left behind it.

12. Each time you breathe out, make a soft humming sound that lasts as long as your breath. Hear this. Then stop making it with your voice and just make it silently

in your mind. Then stop that too, and listen.

13. Rest your eyes for a minute. Check out the back of your eyelids.

14. As you eat, watch your hands.

15. Walk, very slowly, around the room. Pay attention to your body, how it feels. Then sit down and move your hands slowly in front of you. Put them in different positions. Sense the space between and around them. Then let them rest in your lap, close your eyes and sigh. Long, slow, deep.

16. Close your eyes. Watch your thoughts go by like clouds, just passing. Or see yourself as a hollow tube through which your thoughts and senses pass. In one end and out the other. Just watch them going through.

17. Look at the sky now and then.

Chapter Six

Allowing Mind To Be:
The Basic Practice
of Formal Meditation

"Quit trying.
Quit trying not to try.
Quit quitting."
Zen

Free mind   Simply stated, the basic practice of formal meditation is
to let your mind be. It is the utmost of permissiveness, in
which you turn loose the reins with which you have been
commandeering your mind, and for a little while, allow it to
be free. Before trying any of the meditation forms described
later in this book, gain some careful experience with this one.

I.
At a regular time you've set aside, or whenever you
have a free moment, find a fairly quiet place and sit down.
On the floor or in a chair, eyes open or closed, get
comfortable.

II.
Take a few deep breaths, sensing brightness and vigor
like waking-fresh-morning air as you breathe in. And as you
breathe out, relax your body, letting go as with a deep sigh.

III.
Relax your shoulders. Let them be loose. Allow the lines
in your forehead to smooth out. Let your jaw muscles go.
Relax the muscles of your stomach, so your belly just flops
out. Slowly scan your body, and wherever you feel
tightness, let go.

IV.
Let your breathing relax, slowly, gently, sensing deeper
relaxation each time you breathe out.

V.
Do nothing special anymore. Just relax and be.

VI.
Give your mind total permission to be or to do whatever
it wants. *Absolute* permission. Have no objective for your
mind during this time. Expect nothing from it. Just let it be.
There is nothing, *nothing* to be achieved.

VII.
If your mind wants to get quiet, allow it to do so. If it
wants to be noisy, let it. If it wants to become preoccupied
with the sounds or sights or smells or feelings around you or
within you, say "O.K." If you aren't trying to pay attention
to anything in particular, there can be no such thing as a

distraction. Just go wherever your mind goes. If your mind wants to pay attention to something, let it. If it wants to worry or get nervous or sad, bored or angry, empty or hopeful or dictatorial, let it. If it wants to pray, let it. If it wants to think great thoughts, or stupid thoughts, or thoughts about meditation, or thoughts about what you ought to be doing instead of meditating, permit it. Even if it wants to struggle and fight against itself, let it. No exceptions. No restrictions. Just relax and go with it.

VIII.

Don't worry about how much time you're immediately aware as compared to when you're "off" somewhere. If your attention gets carried off, that's fine. Allow it. When you realize attention has been carried off, kidnaped by something, just relax again. At the most, take a deep breath and just relax.

IX.

When the time is up, or when you've had enough, stop. (How crazy! When you've had enough of letting yourself be, you can stop and go back to trying to be in control again.) Let the stopping be slow and gentle; take your time.

X.

If some feelings of openness or peace linger in you for a while, that's great. Let them come along with you as you move into your business. Just don't try to hold them or freeze them. Simply be open to them for as long as they are there.

The difficulty of simplicity

That's all there is to it. Simple and easy, right? Well, it is simple, but it may not be so easy. Sometimes it's not easy just because it *is* so simple. Being so used to complexity, we have some difficulty trying to hang out with simplicity. All sorts of things seem to get in the way.

You may try to sit there and find it just impossible. Itches and jitters, fidgits and agitations. Or maybe some problem in which you're so deeply enmeshed that you can't just sit and watch it. Or maybe your identity is determined by working to improve yourself. In which case letting yourself be will constitute a real threat. Or maybe you feel it is somehow selfish or unjust to be taking time for yourself when there's work to be done or when you really should be spending more time with the kids or whatever. Or maybe it just doesn't seem right to be making peace with yourself when there's so much suffering in the world. Or perhaps you have fallen prey to the American myth that there's something basically bad about feeling good.

For whatever reason, if you have a hard time with the basic practice there is no need to feel defective. I've been meditating for years and it's still more the exception than the rule that I can just hang out with simplicity. *It is important to permit oneself to have the problems one has.*

The rest of this book, in its entirety, is devoted to the fact that simplicity is so difficult. You can move through the suggestions and practices herein and perhaps find something which is helpful. Or you can, without regret, forget all about formal meditation and stick with a more informal approach. Or forget about meditation entirely and simply live your life the best way you can. Which is the best kind of meditation anyway. Remember that just because meditation is an "in" thing is no reason you should do it. If you are able to accept yourself and be aware, as you are, don't mess with it by trying to collect some fancy new techniques.

Similarly, if it is possible for you to stay with the simplicity of the basic practice, for heaven's sake don't go charging through the complexity of the rest of this book in the hopes of finding something "better." If the basic practice feels all right to you, celebrate. And save the rest of the book for another time. And hope that time never comes.

The fear of letting be

Before moving on into greater complexity, there are a few more questions to be answered about the basic practice. They all boil down to what it really means to let oneself be.

"If I really let myself be, does that mean I give in to every impulse? Or that I stray toward what I know to be wrong just because I have an inclination to do so? Do I stop striving for the good, quit trying to improve my life and the lives of those around me? Do I just throw all my controls away and let what happens happen? Should I never struggle with a decision or wrestle with my circumstances?"

Such questions are normal and understandable, but they come out of the crazy assumption that in order to let ourselves be we must stifle conscience or vigor or some other part of ourselves. But to stifle any of these is most certainly *not* letting oneself be. If letting be results in wishy-washiness, a loss of morality or lazy passivity,[1] then it has been grossly abused and misunderstood. Letting be means to let be. To go ahead and live the best way one can, as morally and constructively and dynamically as one can. Letting be means neither to add nor subtract anything from this.

A related question arises for those who deeply mistrust their own nature or who believe in an autonomous power of evil at work in the world. "If I relax and let be; if I truly open to what is, what will prevent me from being overtaken by the demons within myself or the power of Satan from without?" The answer is similar. There is nothing in letting be which says you should kill your fears or your needs for protection. Protect yourself in the best way you can; the way you normally would. Do your best. Then, because you are wise enough to know you can do no more, *then* relax and accept.

For those who fear their own internal demons, this means that normal repression and impulse controls are permitted to go on in meditation in the same way they normally do. They are neither intentionally increased nor decreased. They are not even sought out. They are simply seen and allowed whenever they come into awareness.

For those who fear some external power of evil, this means that normal safeguards are taken. Usually meditation will be preceded by a prayer for protection and guidance. And when fear occurs during meditation, more prayer will happen. An attitude of goodness and purity will be nurtured. I am not suggesting that you should or should not do these things, but am simply indicating that they are normally what happens when there is fear of evil. Just let them be.

Repressing less

As time goes on and the relaxation of meditation deepens, what used to be normal protections may begin to lessen. You'll find that you're not repressing so much, not so concerned about bad things happening, and that you're immediately aware more of the time. This is the result of what I consider to be a very natural process of healing and growth.

One's basic trust in the benevolent processes of life becomes deeper, more certain. And then the layers of defensiveness-against-what-is begin to peel off. The important thing is not to try to push this process. It will become painful and distorted if you try to rush it. Allowed to proceed at its own pace, it will be gentle. It will happen as you are ready for it to happen, and there is no need to do anything special about it.

A gift of healing

If healing happens, it will not be the doing of your hands. If growth takes place, it will not be because you engineered it. Your role is to permit these processes to occur, as they will. To be awake, actively living in the midst of them. Your hands and your will dancing effectively and beautifully within your ongoing living. Free of mastery and meddling because your eyes are open.

1. See appendix, p. 161.

Mind and Me

A separate observer

There you are, sitting comfortably, "trying" to let yourself be who you are. Giving your mind permission. You quickly sense "Here I am, watching, and there's my mind, being watched." This is the same old crazy separate observer business we discussed in connection with informal meditation. It's also a characteristic part of the way we normally view ourselves. It was there all the time. Meditation just brought it to light.

Whenever you think of controlling your mind, or improving it or using it, you're saying there's you and there's your mind. An arbitrary distinction to say the least, but we do it all the time. It's the same when I say "my body," "my behavior," "my senses." There is this ongoing feeling of and belief in a "me" which possesses all these things. But we're never quite sure who or what this "me" really is.

Take a few minutes to watch your mind very carefully. Really see what's going on in there. Then ask yourself who's watching. Try to answer it any way you can; intellectually, experientially, visually. No matter how you try, the paradoxes and convolutions are mind-boggling.

Perhaps the only real sanity of the "mind and me" dichotomy is to realize that one is *not* precisely one's mind, nor body, nor senses, nor behavior. So that though I may not have an understanding of who "I" really am, at least I know some things "I" am not.

It may be a little crazy to sit there and sense that we are separate from our minds, but that's what is liable to happen. And hopefully we shall not try to fix it. It is best to accept it as it is and go with it. This means that most of us will begin meditation with a sense of being related to our minds in some way or another.

Usually this relationship is a rather uncomfortable one,

fraught with considerable conflict. Let's say I don't like what
my mind is doing, so I try to control it. It doesn't like being
controlled, so it rebels. That makes me want to control it
more, and on it goes.

Mind as roommate

In meditation, when you and your mind are at close
quarters, these conflicts can become quite fearsome. In most
of daily living, when awareness is dulled, the mind runs
along, doing its thing while you do yours. You only become
aware of your mind for short moments when something
specially good or bad happens. It's as if you and your mind
lived in next-door apartments and met in the hall now and
then. But in meditation, it's as if you and your mind were
roommates. And in that closeness you have to find a way of
living together in peace. Which means you have to tolerate
some of your mind's irritating habits, and it has to tolerate
yours.

Your tendency will be to try to force your mind to
behave. Make it fit an image of what you want it to be. Try
to get it to meet your expectations. But as anyone who has
ever had a roommate knows, this won't work. Because your
mind won't like it. And chances are it won't put up with it.
If you persist in your authority there will be some heavy
fighting in store, and someone is likely to get hurt.

What we really want with our minds is peace. We don't
want to stifle our minds. Not really. We want them to be
energetic, vibrant and free. We just want them to stop
hassling us so much, and we want to stop hassling them so
much. What we really want is to come back to a kind of
primeval acceptance of each other, where mutual love and
trust allow freedom for both. And most of all, freedom for
awareness.

But one can't even begin to experience something of
this sort when the mind is off somewhere making noise and
raising dust just to feel important and to keep your identity
solid. Nor can this be experienced when you are preoccupied
with trying to control your mind. In order to come to an
initial detente, things somehow have to relax. The dust must
settle a bit. There's got to be a little breathing space.

It would be nice, ideal, if you could be very tolerant
with your roommate. Let your mind act up for a while, until
it gets tired and settles down by itself. Sometimes you can do
this. Sometimes you find yourself being very accepting, and
then things become peaceful, all by themselves. But there are
other times. Times when either you or your mind, or both of
you, are so offensive and irritating that a battle simply must
take place.

Mind as beast

It may seem like your mind is a beast which absolutely
must be tamed before you can trust it. Zen Buddhism has a
delightful series of pictures in which the mind is portrayed
as a wild ox. There's a similar diagram in the Tibetan
tradition, which pictures the mind as a wild elephant. Both
of these describe the process through which the mind is
captured and tamed.

First of all, the beast must be found, and that may take
some doing. Once found, it must somehow be caught. What

For a long time then, your mind charges off, pulling
you along behind, and all you can do is try not to let go.
Finally, the beast gets tired and slows down. Then you can
regain your balance and walk along beside it. This is a very
important time, when trust develops. From there, the
pictures say, one can move ahead and lead the mind
comfortably. It has been domesticated. But this is not the
end. The relationship deepens, until the mind does not need
to be led at all. Nobody is leading or holding anything. The

rope is unnecessary. Mind and me move together, rest together, support each other, until finally, in union, the separation is no more. At this point in the story, my words must stop. From here on out, words don't work.

I have my own image of mind-as-beast, which differs somewhat from those of the east. In my pictures, the mind is a dog, and it's already domesticated. No need to catch it. We've done that a long time ago, in our normal western upbringing. And we're used to leading it. Or at least trying to. So when we encounter the mind, it is already on a leash. And we're already pulling on it.

For some people, mind is like a puppy, frolicking along at the end of its leash, not really clear as to how to follow, but trying just the same. For others, mind is like a well-trained police dog, disciplined and capable of great fierceness. You pick your own species. Poodle, Afghan, Basset Hound?

What we do in meditation is take the collar off. Again, the mind will behave differently for different people when it encounters its newfound freedom. Some, unaccustomed to being without control, will cling close to the master, quiet and shy. Others will burst forth with great energy, cavorting and savoring every inch of freedom. Still others will just lie down and go to sleep. I've never seen it happen, but I suppose some people may fear that their mind might just take off over the hills to parts and places unknown. If this should ever occur, it simply puts one back at the starting point of the Oriental pictures. To find the mind first, and then proceed from there. Remember, this is just a fantasy. Finally, after a while of being without the leash, dog and master come together again. But the master is no longer master. Where there was mastery is now friendship, and where there was a leash is trust. Mind and me together again, at peace.

Perhaps one of these metaphors will fit your experience, and perhaps not. The thing I want to underscore, however, is that nowhere in any of them is any real violence done. There may be plenty of activity, great energy, much conflict and not a few scary moments, but there is no whipping into submission; no abuse, no injury.

Mind as opponent If one wishes to approach the inevitable conflict with mind in such a way as to prevent injury, it is helpful to take another lesson from the east. The oriental martial arts contain rich understandings of how to move into conflict without great destruction. The typical *western* approach to conflict is to charge into it with a bulldozer. Power is what counts. Muscles are tight, adrenalin surges and fists flail wildly. Force meets force in direct and clashing confrontation. When one tackles one's mind in this way, there is both psychological and spiritual bloodshed. And wounds which may take a long time to heal.

Oriental martial arts avoid this. Tai Chi, Kung Fu, Karate, Judo all rely on centered calmness and balance rather than brute force. They use the opponent's own energy to carry him into defeat. Relaxation, not power, is what counts. The most refined of these arts is Aikido, in which there is no attack whatsoever. Total non-aggression which leads the attacker's force gently and easily into quietness. Force, encountering calm, becomes calm.

There is in Aikido a basic body movement called *Tenkan*. It consists of stepping slightly to the side and behind the onrushing opponent, then turning and moving forward *with* his energy. No conflict. Simply going with. My suggestion is to use this kind of strategy when you are in conflict with your mind. Do *Tenkan* with the onrushing thoughts which seek to disrupt your awareness. Step in behind them and move along with them. Allow their own force to carry them into insignificance.

So get off your bulldozer, lay down your club and relax. Be loose, agile, quick to move when mind comes after you. And be very alert, for your mind is sneaky. It is incredibly resourceful in getting you to trap awareness. It wants very much to hold on to that image of big, solid, important, substantial "me."

For example, you're sitting there meditating and you feel it's time to quit. You feel you could just flow from the meditation into the rest of life, awareness free and clear. But here comes mind, sly grin on its face, saying, "Stay longer, sit more, concentrate a little harder, my friend, and you're sure to get even more out of this meditation. You feel good now, right? Well then try a little harder and you'll feel even better." And you are duped. It doesn't sound like such a bad idea, so you go ahead and work harder at it. But now you're expecting to get something out of it and you want to achieve something and you've forgotten all about being who you are, and suddenly it's all "lost." There in the background is mind, polishing your well-preserved identity and chuckling to itself.

Or your mind may say: "Well now, my friend, here you are getting ready to meditate, but you don't really feel like it, do you? You're really tired. You worked hard today. You deserve to take it easy. Now listen to me . . . this meditation business is to let you be who you are, right? Do what comes naturally, right? Well then, why meditate—let's you and me go get stoned." Or, "My, we've had a lot of very fine meditations, haven't we? We're really very spiritually sophisticated. Much better off than those poor souls who don't understand God the way we do."

Mental martial arts

All this trickery is your mind fighting to preserve self-image. And you really need to be very alert to see it coming. Most of the time you won't catch it till it's well under way. That's O.K. The important thing is to catch it sometime, and to have the proper attitude when you do. When you catch your mind in the act of trickery, it will be tempting to hop on your bulldozer, grab a club, and get into a bloody fight which won't do anyone any good. At this time, it can be very helpful to remember some basic attitudes which characterize the oriental martial arts:

1. Honor and Respect

The fight begins with a bow of respect. No name-calling or rushing into it. In meditation, your attitude toward mind should be respectful, honorable and compassionate. No criticism, derogation or contempt.

2. Allowing

Do not attempt to restrict the movements of your opponent. If the mind wishes to come on with great force, allow that. Accept with equanimity whatever mind may present, and go with it.

3. Not Being Driven

Rather than being driven into the conflict by greed or fear or anger, simply be there. No adrenalin. No great expectations. No grasping, pulling, holding or shoving. Simple presence.

4. Flexibility

Bend, moving with the force of mind. Setting up no obstacle, holding no resistance, you flow with the mental energy rather than opposing. Roll with the punches, bend with the wind, and no one will be hurt.

5. Permissiveness

No restriction. Absolute acceptance. Pamper the mind and treat it like a wayward child, lovingly allowing it to stumble over its own feet. Redirecting it only just before it becomes destructive. Make no demands. Even *encourage* the folly of mind. If it wants to obsess you with some thought, say "Go ahead, little mind, obsess away, 'til you've had enough."

6. Elusiveness

Never present a definite target to your mind. Hold no solid image of yourself. Freeze no expectation. Be evanescent, here and there, like wisps of fog. Then there is nothing of substance for your mind to fight.

7. Unilateral Withdrawal

If your mind presses you into a corner, give up. Concede. Lay down your arms. Be totally vulnerable. Expose your soft underbelly. Hand over your wallet. When you are totally naked, totally undefended, the mind has nothing left to fight, and no reason to want to.

8. Alertness

Constantly watch. Attentive always, you are ever prepared to sidestep the mind's attack. When it sneaks up on you, you will see it. When it strikes, you will be gone. Watching, always watching, you will learn to see.

9. Humor

Never heavy. Never taking anything too seriously. Buoyed up by waves of laughter you are free to breathe. When the mind assumes a tragic face, chuckle. When it wears the mask of suffering, smile. When it plays monster, giggle. And when it becomes sentimental, grin. Sooner or

later your mind will see the comedy too, and the two of you
will fall down laughing together.

It is just possible that if the two of you laugh together enough, the entire problem of separate observer will crumble, and the laughing will simply happen.

Part II

Ground Rules for Formal Meditation

"To insure peace of mind ignore the rules and regulations."
George Ade, *Forty Modern Fables*

Chapter Eight

Being Gentle

"For my yoke is easy, and my burden is light."
Matthew 11:30

Above all, be gentle with yourself. Any heavy struggle, any forceful striving or fighting against yourself is likely to push you into even greater attachment and self-importance. Then your attention will be bonded to some task or struggle rather than freed to appreciate awareness. This does not mean that you give in to every whim or that you cast the idea of discipline out the window. That would just be being gentle with your lazy side, and stifling your sense of what needs to be done. You have to be gentle with your *whole* self, and that includes your willful side too; the side that says, "Listen, you, you have to sit there for umpteen minutes every day and meditate or you're not going to get anything out of it." Keep in mind that laziness is not a primary drive. Rather, it is a rebellion against all the demands and expectations that you and others place on yourself. If you can be gentle with the demands, and gentle with the laziness too, there won't be so much need to rebel, and things will calm down considerably. You'll be more free simply to do what needs to be done.

Sometimes, for example, you may not feel like meditating at all. Be gentle with that. Maybe you shouldn't meditate just then. But before you decide to take the day off, listen to the other side. Maybe there's something saying, "You need to do it anyway, whether you feel like it or not." Be gentle with that too. Accept. Allow. If you team up with one side against the other, you will be increasing the struggle. But if you treat both sides with the same acceptance and gentleness, you will be left in the middle, free to do what needs to be done. How then does the decision get made? If you don't freeze anything, the decision will simply be made. Sound difficult? Again, it's something that needs to be experienced rather than figured out, but let me give you an **Gentleness** example. When you sit in meditation, things may start to go **with body** to sleep. Like feet and fingers and knees. Hopefully not your head. When these things start to go to sleep, they tingle and feel numb. Then they begin to *hurt.* And it can all be very distracting. At first when your body starts to hurt, it's best to go ahead and move. Change your position and get more comfortable. That's being gentle. You're hearing a pain-signal from your body and responding to it. Sometime later on though, you may have a sense that it is deeply right just to keep on sitting, right on through the pain. So maybe you listen to that too, and find that you can easily sit still in the midst of the pain. That's being gentle too. You're letting the pain be, and you're letting the sitting still be. Because it seems right and because *it is not a struggle.* It's just something that happens and you allow it. The point is that by being gentle with both sides you do not get caught in the struggle. The two sides work it out, and something feels right and you do it. If you're caught up in the struggle, hassling and fighting with yourself, then you're not being gentle. You're back in the driver's seat, trying to commandeer your mind, and you're just feeding the fire of your own internal argument. So you may have pain and find that you're struggling with it. Then maybe you should move and get rid of the pain. Or you can have pain and find that you're not struggling with it. Then maybe you can just let it be. Both are gentleness. We'll discuss this more when we talk about handling distractions, but I would like to point out here that if you've never had pain without struggling with it, you have a very pleasant surprise awaiting you in meditation. I never understood the difference between pain and suffering until I started to meditate. Pain is just pain. It's a certain kind of sense-stimulus which is really no different from red or soft or loud or bitter. Suffering is the struggle with which we *respond* to pain. The difference is a wondrous thing to experience. But it will never be experienced unless you are gentle with your body.

Gentleness with mind It's just as important, if not more so, to be gentle with your mind. And again I have to repeat that gentleness does not at all mean being passive or lazy. It means hearing the very essence of any struggle and finding some place in the middle of it where you can relax. Gentleness to your mind is that tender, understanding parental attitude that says, "I love you, mind, whatever you do." It's the living out of the Christian Gospel that states, "Just as you are, right now, you are accepted, loved and forgiven." It is also the practice of Buddhist compassion which is the ultimate kind of love. Love with no manipulation whatsoever. No attachment or needing or taking. Total acceptance of what is, including acceptance of any desire you may have to change things. *Total* acceptance. It's very open and spacious and light, this gentleness.

As is the case with pain in the body, mental pain or anguish in meditation is usually a danger signal. At least while you're still a "beginner" at formal meditation. Anxiety, fear or rage probably means you ought to back off and take it easy for a while. Because to push forward would be a struggle. Pushing through into this kind of struggle, when your body or your mind is screaming in agony, can be dangerous. That's how people hurt their bodies and injure their minds. There's no gentleness in pushing yourself through some monstrous struggle in meditation. That's self-serving egocentric bulldozering, and it's dangerous. But again, with some practice in letting yourself be in meditation, there will be times when you encounter some fear or sadness or some other mental pain and it just feels deeply right to sit on through it, go through it, see it through, let it come and let it pass while you neither grab for it nor flee from it. That kind of right feeling comes when there's no struggle.

When there's fear or pain but there's no struggle, then

you can go ahead and be with the discomfort and it's all gentle from your side, and that's just fine. Just don't get impatient with yourself and try to fight your way through a struggle. If you're gentle, and if you wait long enough, the no-struggle times will come, of their own accord. Then there can be mental pain without suffering, just as there can be physical pain without suffering. And it can all be gentle. Understanding this is important. It even makes *some* sense out of the crazy self-abusing things that some saints and other spiritual athletes have reportedly done to themselves. You know that lying on a bed of nails is probably just some kind of self-serving masochism. It would be if you or I did it. But it's *possible* that just *maybe* it's different for the guy who's doing it. It just *might* be real gentleness. You and I will never know. We can only hope he does.

If you're left with the feeling that *none* of this makes sense and you're not sure what to do when you encounter pain or anxiety, here's the answer, simple and clear: When your body hurts, move it so that it's comfortable. When your mind hurts or gets scared, don't panic and run away, but simply back off a little, take a break, or change your meditative tactics. The subtleties of gentleness will come clear as they need to. In the meantime, just *take it easy on yourself*.

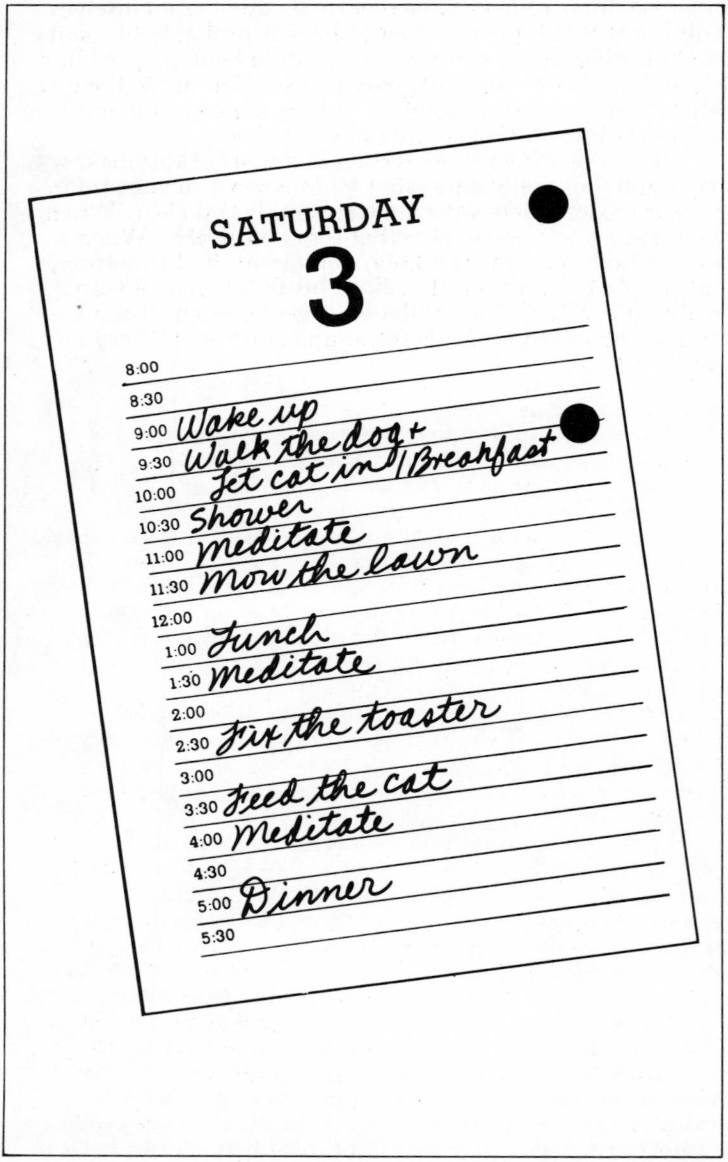
SATURDAY
3
8:00
8:30
9:00 Wake up
9:30 Walk the dog +
Let cat in / Breakfast
10:00
10:30 Shower
11:00 Meditate
11:30 Mow the lawn
12:00
1:00 Lunch
1:30 Meditate
2:00
2:30 Fix the toaster
3:00
3:30 Feed the cat
4:00 Meditate
4:30
5:00 Dinner
5:30

Chapter Nine

Time

Non multa sed multum.
(Not quantity but quality.)

When   When to meditate, how often and for how long? The quickest and best answer is that you meditate when it feels right to, as frequently as you need to, for as long as is necessary. If you can really be in gentle touch with your needs, this answer is sufficient. But for most of us it's not quite enough.

Start with when to meditate. Or perhaps when not to. Many traditions say you shouldn't try to meditate on a full stomach. After you eat, your body routes much of your blood supply to the digestive system, and for a while your brain is working without much energy reserve. So you may alter your consciousness all right. Right to sleep. And you may come away with a feeling that meditation is a very dull undertaking. On the other hand, I don't see what real harm it could do. If you are moving to accept yourself, I suspect that acceptance of a full stomach and sleepiness would be very good practice.

The same applies to meditation when your mind is befogged with alcohol, tobacco or other chemicals. If the chemical is a depressant, everything will be quite dull. If it is a stimulant, you can forget getting quiet. Sharp keen awareness is difficult if your consciousness has been dulled by chemicals, fatigue or anything else. But of course if you're addicted, you have to begin where you are and do the best you can. We all begin with some kind of addiction which dulls awareness. If it's not chemicals or overeating, then it's some other favorite preoccupation or activity in which we habitually "lose" ourselves.

Early morning is a nice and natural meditation time for many people. If you meditate twice a day, before supper is a good second time. Or before bed. The latter may interfere a bit with sleeping habits, but that's something which shouldn't cause much difficulty.

I personally found that meditation seemed quite different depending on what time of day I "did" it. The morning was "harder" somehow at the beginning, because there seemed to be all sorts of obsessive thoughts left over from the night. The afternoon was easier because I was a little tired and ready to relax and take it easy. Both were important in their way. Other people have different experiences. The important thing is to find some kind of schedule that will fit into your daily routine without too much disruption and without being too special. One man I know experimented with all sorts of times and finally settled on between 12:00 and 2:00 A.M. He'd go to sleep at a normal hour, wake up at midnight, meditate, and go back to sleep. Now he's been doing this for a couple years and it works out fine for him. But at the beginning, do plan some kind of schedule, so there really is a place in your life for meditation. Don't just leave it to chance or your mind will get the better of you. Remember, your mind is going to go

Excuses through some changes. It may start out saying, "My, how very interesting all this meditation business is." But pretty soon it will begin to discover that what meditation is doing is letting things be quiet. And it doesn't want to be quiet. And it will say, "Hey, now, wait just a minute. What's happening here?" Then it will get very sneaky and you'll find yourself coming up with all sorts of excuses. "I'm too tired to meditate." "There's just too much to do." Or some really crazy ones like "There's too much on my mind," or "I'm too upset to meditate." These mental diversions are just easier to handle if you have a schedule—a time set aside for meditation. But don't make a big discipline-deal out of it.

Many people have said to me, "With my busy schedule, I just don't have time to meditate." My response is, "Fine, then don't." If they are comfortable with that, great. But many will say, "No, I really do want to meditate, I really do. I just don't have the time." Now that *is* a cop-out. Because if you really want to, there's plenty of time. After all, we do watch TV or read or do more work than we need to, or go to the bathroom or wait for the bus or spend time gossiping with the neighbors. Nobody is too busy. There's always a few minutes a day that can be scared up. Lack of time can never be an excuse. Besides, there's no reason for excuses. Meditation is not something you *should* do anyway. You do it because you need to or really want to. Either you want to or you don't. There's no reason you have to kid yourself or make excuses. There are many times when you won't feel like meditating, when you simply don't want to. It may be because you pushed yourself too much the last time, or because your mind is getting scared of being quiet and losing your self-image or some other reason. It's much better to be honest about it. If you don't feel like meditating, simply don't make a hassle of it with convoluted excuses. Try to keep a schedule of meditation, and make it reasonably regular, but don't make it a crusade of the conscience.

How Often Another question that is especially important for those
How Long beginning meditation is what the frequency and length of meditation should be. I feel strongly that you should not push yourself beyond what feels comfortable, especially at the beginning. This may mean, for some people, that formal meditation only lasts a couple of minutes. It's not uncommon to start feeling quite anxious when you're just sitting and not doing anything. If you feel that way, then if you push yourself to sit longer, meditation may wind up being a very unpleasant experience. My suggestion is to begin with no longer than five minutes once or twice a day. Work it into your schedule somewhere conveniently. Pretty soon, you'll find yourself spontaneously extending the periods as comfort allows. A friend of mine started out meditating during the time it took her water to boil for

morning tea. After a while, that was too short and she had to restructure her schedule. But for the beginning it had worked beautifully. *Don't* go over about a half hour at the beginning, even if you're tempted. Get some experience under your belt. Take it easy. Some people with whom I've worked started out meditating for a short time. Then, because it felt so good somehow, they quickly moved to periods of one or two hours several times a day. What they wound up doing, very soon, was using meditation as a way of escaping from "real life." They altered their consciousness, and found they liked it better "there" than "here." Some of them had a bit of trouble getting "back." Extended periods such as these should be for those who have a great deal of experience or *very* competent guidance. Use your common sense.

After two or three weeks of regular practice find a time with which you're comfortable, preferably between five and thirty minutes once or twice a day. Short periods regularly are much better than extended periods now and then. Don't become a fanatic in any way. Fanaticism is another word for trapped awareness. The total number of hours you log in formal meditation means nothing. The quality of that meditation, and, more importantly, how clear and free your awareness is the *rest* of the time—*that's* what really counts.

You can check your time in a variety of ways. If you have the flexibility, you can just stop whenever it seems right to—when you've had enough. This is fine at the beginning. Later on, it may feel right to keep meditating until you've gone through that "I've had enough" feeling and *then* stop. But that's something you should let happen spontaneously. Don't push it. If you've set aside a certain amount of time, you can tell your own internal clock to let you know when time's up. It will be amazingly accurate if you trust it. Or you can sneak glances at your watch. This can create some "distractions" about how fast or slow the time is going, but you can let go of these ideas easily. Don't set an alarm clock that you have to jump up and turn off. You want to come "out" of meditation loosely, not with a jolt. A timer with a gentle "ding" would be fine. Some people light a stick of incense and meditate till it's burned down. Work out some easy no-big-deal way of doing it. And remember to give yourself time both at the beginning and at the end to stretch, breathe and relax. At the end, you may also want to leave some time to make a few notes.

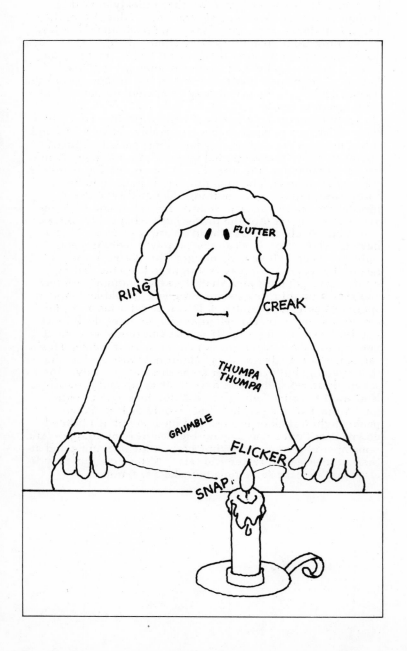

Chapter Ten

Place

"With an host of furious fancies
Whereof I am commander,
With a burning spear, and a horse of air,
To the wilderness I wander.
By a knight of ghosts and shadows
I summoned am to tourney
Ten leagues beyond the wide world's end.
Methinks it is no journey."

Anonymous,
Tom O'Bedlam

Idealizing   If your fantasies are like mine, you think of ideal
meditation as taking place on a beautiful spring or fall
morning, outdoors, under a very accepting tree, on a
mountain, preferably in view of the sea, probably
somewhere near Big Sur in California (where all the good
meditation occurs) with no flies buzzing or mosquitoes
imposing their little wills upon your body, and with the
birds singing a spiritual mantra somewhere in the
background. The air is filled with the natural incense of
flowers or pine trees, and the breeze strokes your skin ever
so gently.

Nice work if you can get it. I've never meditated in that
kind of setting. The closest I came to Big Sur was sitting
crosslegged in a dumpy motel room in Anaheim. And I
meditated once in the Arizona desert. The motel room
meditation went well, because I was busy at a conference and
had to squeeze in the meditation-time, so it wasn't anything
special, and therefore was good. The meditation in the desert
wasn't the best because I got very hung up in thinking how
beautiful it all was and what an ideal place to meditate.
Never really did get around to meditating. Again, if you're
like most of us, the fantasy of an ideal setting for meditation
will remain just that—a fantasy. What we actually have to
contend with is a noisy house or apartment, with other
people running around, jabbering, jiggling the floor,
flushing toilets, screeching brakes, honking horns. And the
flies and mosquitoes won't be at all considerate.

Which, I think, is just great. Because it is when your
mind comes home after being carried off by some
"distraction" that you can really sense being aware. Without
"distractions," that opportunity would never occur. Besides,
if one is attempting to be open to what is, "distractions" are
simply part of it all.

It's nice to have a quiet place to meditate, but it's not
necessary. And certainly it's easier when there are less
distractions, but it's a mistake to get the idea that it must be
quiet. A couple of years ago I fell into that. It seemed I
couldn't meditate because the kids were always running

around and making noise. I'd get angry with them for "interfering" (with what?) and yell at them, and then I'd feel guilty, and that would make more noise inside me, and it kept getting all agitated and crawly instead of peaceful and accepting.

So I decided to get up earlier in the morning. While the little darlings were still asleep. I'd set the alarm for some ridiculously masochistic hour, far before dawn, and then sneak down the stairs to meditate. But through those mystical powers for innocent treachery that only children have, the kids started getting up earlier too. No matter how quiet and early I was, I'd be greeted by one or more smiling morning faces.

So I tried staying up later. Meditate after the little people had retired for the night. But by then I was so tired from my early risings that as soon as I'd sit down to meditate I'd go to sleep.

Perseverance. Finally I laid claim to a corner of the basement, got hammer and nails, and built myself a real live meditation room. Just big enough for yoga, with soundproofing, cushions, candles and the works. It was finally going to be quiet. When it was finished, I entered and sat down with great hopes and no little ceremony. But it was stuffy. And too hot. And there still was noise. My jaw joint, I noticed, creaked. And then there was my breathing, sounding like a DC-6 rhythmically indecisive as to whether to take off or land. My ears reverberated with a myriad of ringings, and my skull produced all manner of tick-ticks and crunches. I was more "distracted" than ever.

Carrying Noise/ Carrying Silence

It finally dawned on me that the problem was not the environment. The problem was within me. I was distracting myself, being so selective about what I wanted to pay attention to and what I did not that I was most effectively preventing myself from meditating. I was carrying the noise inside me wherever I went. I realized that if that were true, then I must be carrying quietness within me too. And that made it possible to open. To let all the distractions be, allow them to come in to consciousness and pass on out again without my being kidnaped by them. After that, I was able to sit down in the middle of the living room, while the kids were running around, and pretty much accept. There's still a level of noise that I can't just accept, but most of the time, it's fine. And what's nice about it is that the kids started to come up and sit down with me for a while during my meditations. That's nice.

The how

Maybe it's necessary for some of us to go through all these geographic escapades before we finally believe that where we meditate isn't anywhere near as important as how. I know one woman who resorted in despair to the bathroom to get some quiet. She didn't feel the vibrations were very good in there, sitting on the john and trying to let herself be. And even then the kids kept pounding on the door with "Mommy, when are you going to be finished?" Perhaps it's necessary. Somehow we have to learn that we carry our noise around with us. And our quiet too.

There is one good thing about having a certain place to meditate. If you don't use it for any other activity, just going there will help put you in an open and receptive frame of mind. Many houses in other countries, and a few in this one, have special places set aside for prayer and meditation. You can do this too. Just take an unused corner somewhere, put a little table there, maybe with flowers or a candle, and a cushion, and you're all set. But don't get carried away with it as I did. Don't make it too special or heap too many expectations on it, or you'll find your attention getting glued to the place and how to make it nicer and how wonderful it is or maybe it would be better with the table over there . . . And then you won't have any time or energy left for meditation.

An out-of-doors place, if the weather permits, or next to an open window, is very helpful. Even if the weather doesn't permit, you might give it a try. It's beyond words to bundle up in a blanket and let the snow fall on you for a while, or to feel a warm summer rain tapping your shoulders. Being outdoors, or close to it by a window, will do wonders if you find sleepiness a problem. It has always seemed important to me to have some connection with the ouside when I meditate, even if it's only sunlight, a breeze, or a glimpse of the sky. That's just one of my enjoyable attachments.

If you have some choice of places, count yourself as fortunate and proceed to select the one in which you can feel most *comfortable*, both physically and mentally. Just remember, comfort does not mean getting lazy or lethargic. It means being able to be alert and relaxed at the same time.

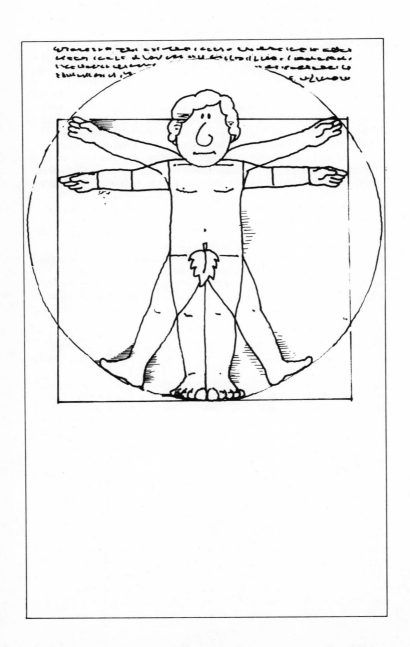

Chapter Eleven

Body

"But O the ship, the immortal ship!
   O ship aboard the ship!
O ship of the body—ship of the soul
   —voyaging, voyaging, voyaging."
Walt Whitman,
Leaves of Grass

Your body is another kind of environment. The internal milieu. If you can allow your body to relax, your mind will relax. It's as simple as that. If you feel anxious, try relaxing all the muscle groups in your body, one by one. When they're all loose and easy, look around for the anxiety you felt. It will be gone. For a while. When it returns, look over your body and you will find some tension. That's how close body and mind are related. They are in large part reflections of each other.

Because of this intimate relationship, I think it is very important to take some time for the body both before and after formal meditation, to relax, to breathe, and, most of all, get comfortable. This means to find the right position.

Posture   It may seem like I make a big deal out of position and posture, but remember that it's all for comfort and naturalness, staying bright and alert and relaxed. If you can do this lounging back with your feet up on the desk, great. Right now if I slouch or lie down to meditate, I usually go to sleep. Or at least my awareness gets foggy.

Meditation has helped me discover that the most relaxing, refreshing and energizing posture for me is to sit up straight. Always before when I was tired or bored or sad, it seemed to make sense to slouch. So I did a lot of slouching. What I didn't realize was that the position wasn't doing anything to make me feel better; it was just *expressing* how I felt. And so it helped me *continue* to feel tired or bored or sad. What I discovered was that the worse I felt, the more helpful it was to sit up straight, with my head high, my lungs filled with air, and my shoulders relaxed. *All* my muscles relaxed.

Believe it or not, you can relax all your muscles and still remain sitting up straight. Look at how a little child sits. When my kids were toddlers I would just marvel at how absolutely straight their backs were when they sat down. And it's kind of sad, as the years pass, to see the slump begin. What kind of weight is it that brings those little shoulders down? At any rate, sitting up very straight is a natural thing to do, and it is the most comfortable of positions. But for us older adult grown-up types who've forgotten how, it takes some practice. Like most things having to do with meditation, it's more of an unlearning of how not to than a learning of how to.

It takes a bit of a search to find the right position in which you can sit up straight and still relax completely. I remember one man who came to the first meeting of a meditation group, got himself situated in a nice crosslegged position on the floor and proceeded to relax. He'd neglected to find the right position for his spine, and as his muscles relaxed, he started to slump forward. When he got very relaxed he wound up with his face on the floor. Which is quite a trick when you're sitting cross-legged.

Spine Your spine is built in such a way that it can support itself with little or no muscular effort. The vertebrae in your spine are round flat bones which can stack up like checkers and stay there if you arrange them correctly. It's a little more difficult than checkers, because some of the vertebrae are slanted a bit on the tops and bottoms. These slants result in three normal curves in your spine which need to be allowed.

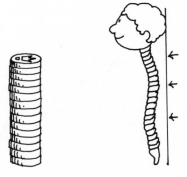

Sitting up straight does not mean your spine gets straight like a ruler. You'd get pretty tired pretty fast that way. You have to let it curve in its natural way, not too little and not too much. If you can get the lower back (lumbar area) to curve in the proper amount, the other curves will come naturally. You can feel the right amount of this curve by lying flat on the floor or standing straight up against a wall. If you pass your hand behind your low back, about waist level, you'll feel some space between you and the floor or the wall. That's where your natural lumbar curve should be. There will also be a little space behind your neck (the cervical curve). In both cases, the curve will probably be a little less than the thickness of your hand. This will give you an idea of what the curve is like naturally. Another way is to stand up straight and clasp your hands together behind your back, up against the lumbar area. Take a deep breath. Feel the curve go in? That's about right. When you exhale, keep the curve in rather than slouching forward. Just let the weight of your shoulders and chest settle down onto that curve. Let your stomach muscles go loose, let your stomach protrude. No tenseness. Try this a couple times and you'll find a position that feels "right." Then you will be standing straight. Try to keep that "right" feeling as you sit down. If you do this in public there'll be a few raised eyebrows. You look a little bit like you're afraid of sitting in something. But it will feel *good*. If it doesn't feel good, you don't have it right. If you lose the right position somewhere between standing up and sitting down, you may be able to find it again by getting your butt firmly planted and swaying your trunk around in ever-decreasing circles, till your spine finally settles into that right-feeling position.

That right feeling is your most important help in finding the proper position. When you find it, you'll know it, and you'll know it for sure. Trust it. Sometimes in meditation you realize you've found it and it feels so perfect you're afraid to move a single muscle lest you disturb it. That's great! It takes some time, so have patience.

Once you've got the spine straight, *relax your shoulders.* Just let your shoulder muscles go. You don't need to keep them pulled back or tense at all. If your spine is O.K. you can let these big shoulder muscles relax and your posture will be just fine. After you've meditated for a while, you may find you've begun to slouch. And you don't want to disturb your meditation with a major position change. In this case, I've found it helpful to imagine that my head is being pulled straight up—as if by a cord attached to some great winch in the sky.

It just gently straightens my spine by pulling up on my head. You can try it if you like.

Here I am writing paragraph after paragraph about how to find our spines' "natural" position. It's ironic that we have to go through so much rigmarole to find out what is just natural and spontaneous. But that's what meditation is all about. If we can allow our bodies to find their natural state, there's a chance that maybe we can allow our minds to do the same.

Reminder: I made a big deal of this finding the proper spine position. Don't *you* make a big deal of it or you'll find you've used up all your meditation time fiddling around with posture. Sit down, get it so it feels O.K., then forget it and get on with just being aware. Next time it may be easier.

Sitting Some good yogis like to sit on the plain hard floor and get into a fancy crosslegged position with the spine just right. That *does* take practice. You're much better off to begin with sitting either on a chair or crosslegged on the floor with your buttocks on a cushion. There are more specifics about this. Those two little bones that you sit on are the ischial tuberosities. Better to call them sitting bones. They're the ones which begin to hurt after you've sat a long time on a hard surface. (Unless you're especially well endowed with cushioning of your own—in which case you might never discover their whereabouts.) Sometime, preferably in private, poke around and find them. They're really not very big but they are what you ought to be sitting on. That's what they're there for. When we slouch back on a chair, we're usually sitting more on the lower part of our spines. Other times we may be sitting more on the backs of our thighs. But those sitting bones are made for sitting on, and that's what we ought to do.

If you choose a chair, pick a straight upright one. Nothing overstuffed or cushiony. It should be high enough so that your knees are at or below the level of your sitting bones. Put both feet squarely on the floor and sit up straight. In order to sit on those bones you'll find you have to sit toward the front of the chair. As a matter of fact, those bones ought to be perched right on the very edge for the best posture. So you can't lean back.

If you sit on the floor you should have a *very firm* cushion that will hold your bottom 3 to 6 inches off the floor. It is important that the cushion be firm. Otherwise it will get all squishy and you won't know where your sitting bones are. A blanket rolled up *very* tightly will do. I use a kapok life-preserver cushion folded in half. (It also helps when I get that sinking feeling in meditation.) Or you can sit on a couple of books (preferably highly spiritual books), or make a little bench out of wood. Most of the cotton or foam pillows available are just too soft and don't hold you up far enough. Experiment. You can buy a Zen meditation pillow called a zafu if you can avoid feeling important because you have it. If you make a cushion, use kapok for the stuffing and pack it tightly.

When you use a cushion, your sitting bones again should be perched right on the edge. Sit too far back and it will be impossible to get the spine right. Whether in a chair or on the floor, let your stomach flop out kind of loosely in the front. That will also help you get the lumbar curve right. Sometimes I get situated comfortably and suddenly realize my stomach muscles are tight as a drum. I feel as though if I let them go either I wouldn't be able to breath or I'd topple over. So I have to shift around again to let them relax. It's good to do lots of shifting and fidgeting before meditation. Get it all taken care of then, so you can forget it while you're meditating.

Legs and feet

Now, in the midst of all this, we have to figure out what to do with our appendages. Take the legs first. If you're in a chair, there's no problem. Just get them comfortable with feet on the floor. If you're on the floor, there are more problems. I can remember several times when I used up all my meditation time just fiddling around with my legs—trying to find a good position. Ideally, if you've got the right kind of cushions and you're sitting correctly, your crossed legs should bear almost no weight at all. It's all absorbed by those ischial tuberosities. Probably just crossing your legs Indian-style will work best at the beginning. This means that your ankles or shins will be crossed, with the sides of your feet on the floor, and your knees up off the ground a bit. That's fine if it's comfortable.

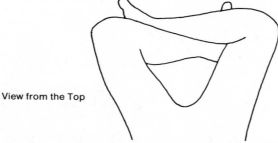

View from the Top

Another position is to bring one heel right up under the crotch and rest the other foot either on the floor in front or up on the shin or thigh of your other leg. This gets your knees on the ground, and it may feel better.

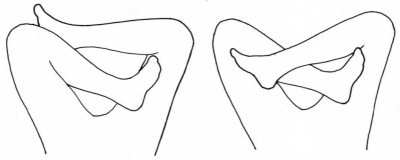

This gets close to yoga positions, the most excruciating of which is the lotus. Why they named such a painful position after such a lovely flower I'll never understand. As near as I can figure out, there are only two advantages to it. One is that if you go "far, far out" in meditation (which isn't the kind of meditation we're talking about anyway), it will keep you from toppling over. The other is that once you've got them there, they lock in and stay there, and you can forget them. Except that they hurt. At least mine do. If you can get into the lotus *comfortably*, do it. If you can't, don't worry about it. If there's one thing I'm firmly convinced of, it's that the quality of meditation is not ultimately determined by the position of one's legs. Again, the hallmark is to find a position which feels *comfortable* and *natural*. You will find that different positions of the legs are needed at different times. Be flexible. Don't force anything! One other option, which I find very refreshing at times, is to assume a kneeling position with your cushion resting either on the floor with your legs back at the sides of it, or put the cushion right on your calves and sit on it. Again, experiment and find comfort.

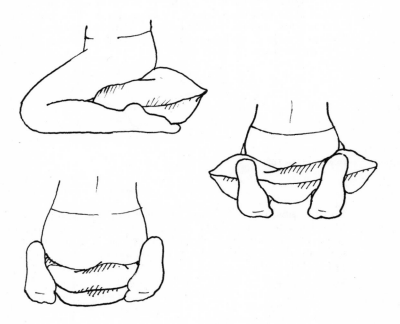

Arms and hands

Now for the hands and arms. Remember, we've let the shoulders go, so they're just flopping around like they ought to. But what about those hands? You have to put them somewhere. Usually, I just rest them on my knees—plant them there and let my arms relax. Sometimes, though, it seems important to do something a little more sophisticated or symbolic with them. We use our hands to express ourselves so much that their positions actually influence how we feel. Try this: Make fists with both hands and hold them up in front of you. Sense how you feel. Then slowly open them, palms outstretched, facing up. What is your feeling now? Then bring them back toward you—palms facing away from you. What's that like?

So the position of our hands sometimes can help us with our mental attitude. In mystical traditions, there are a wide variety of hand positions, called mudras, which are done for special effects. You can read up on them and experiment if you wish. Our needs here are simply to find some ways of holding our hands that will help with a mental attitude of relaxed alertness. This means that we should put them in some position that is easy to hold (relaxed) yet not sloppy (alert). Again, don't make a big deal of it. I will describe four positions that I have used. You can use these or find your own.

First is simply to rest the hands on the knees, palms down or up. With palms down there is a little more sense of strength and confidence. With palms up, more of a sense of openness and receptivity:

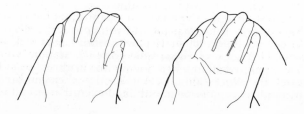

A simple yogic mudra adds just a little alertness when I do it.
The hands are in the same position on the knees, palms up
or down, but the index finger is curved round to touch the
thumb.

Or the hands can be placed in the lap, palms up, one resting
on top of the other, thus:

For a little brigher attention, this position can be modified by
curving the hands a bit more and bringing the tips of the
thumbs together, to form an oval space when viewed from
the front. From your perspective it looks like this:

Again, don't worry about getting your position just as
I've described it. The most important thing is to check out
how it feels. If anything about your position feels awkward,
forced or contrived, switch to something that feels natural to
you. This goes for all aspects of the meditation: your
breathing, whether your eyes are open, closed or at half-
mast, the expression on your face, whether you breath
through your nose or mouth, and even that spinal posture I

spent so much time with. If it really feels more natural to
slouch back or lean against the wall or put your feet up,
fine! Your awareness of what is natural is what counts. In
the beginning, I found it better to slouch. My mind seemed
freer that way, I guess because I was just so used to
slouching. As my meditation experience developed however,
what seemed natural started to change. I began to sit up
straighter and pay more attention to my hands. Now when I
slouch, I get sleepy. This may be your experience as well. Do
not confuse your fantasy-image of what meditation *ought* to
be like with what *you* are really like right now. It is allowing
yourself to be exactly what you are right now that you want.
Growth, or development, or clearer awareness will come if
you stay naturally and spontaneously with who you are.
You can't force it. Keep your grubby hands off yourself.

Relaxing

"Light be the earth upon you, lightly rest."
Euripides, *Alcestis*

The nature of relaxing   We've said before that meditation is relaxed awareness. Relaxation is an important word, with lots of connotations. It means getting your hands off who you are, letting be, stopping struggling, opening, allowing, accepting. It means loosening up in both body and mind, cutting through all the tension, tightness and restriction.

    Right now, make a fist with one hand and tense all the muscles in your arm. It feels tight, as though cords were attached to the bones, muscles and joints, pulling taut, holding hard, frozen, rigid. Now, very slowly, let your hand and arm relax. Feel the tension easing, the cords getting looser, the bones, joints and muscles thawing out and easing. Feel what that process is like.

    We're very familiar with what it feels like to tense up or constrict our muscles. We see that as something we *do*, wilfully, every time we physically act. Relaxing is another process, and also, in a way, it is something we can *do*. We're just not as used to it. If you practice that exercise with your hand and arm, you can learn what the relaxation-process feels like. Then you can scan over your body and "do" it anywhere you feel tension. Let's assume you're sitting relatively at rest right now. Or at least you think you are. Check out your shoulders—the muscles which go from your shoulders to your neck. Relax them. Your shoulders will lower a little. There was tension there which you may not have been aware of. Or think about your jaw muscles, or the muscles that wrinkle your forehead or squint your eyes. Let them go. Feel the difference?

    Relaxing is something we can "do." And if we can "do" it with our bodies, we can also "do" it with our minds. That tense, taut, frozen feeling we get with tightened muscles is mirrored by the tenseness we often feel in our minds. When our minds are tight and constricted, struggling or striving, it feels as if there were cords binding our awareness, holding our thoughts, and restricting the flow of our consciousness. This mirroring of tension is so complete that mental tension is always accompanied by muscular tension somewhere in the body. And if you can allow your muscles to relax, your mind also will be at peace. At least for a while. This is why it's important to pay attention to the body if we want to allow consciousness to be free.

    There are some interesting aspects to this relaxation business. One is that relaxation does not at all mean sleepiness or fogginess. On the contrary, true relaxation means a very bright, clear and open awareness. Rather than going to sleep, we wake up. We have associated awareness with tension for so long that it's hard to see awareness as a function of relaxation. When we say "pay attention!" we usually mean to "focus" attention. Which means to shut out other stimuli—not to be "distracted." That requires energy and it causes conflict and tension.

But relaxation simply means that we *free* awareness. We don't shut out "distractions." We don't try to be selective about what enters awareness. We just open to it all. We relax the barriers we've constructed against "distractions" and allow our awareness to be free. This frees up energy and diminishes conflict and tension. It's not at all like going to sleep. In sleep, our minds work hard to keep consciousness dull and to hold off distractions that might wake us up. Have you ever had a dream that incorporated some real sound, like the alarm clock or telephone? That's your mind *working* to do something with stimuli so you can stay asleep. Lots of work goes on in sleep. And lots of work goes on in our usual daily behavior of *concentrating* on one thing and trying to shut out everything else. There is much less work involved in being openly aware. That's why many people find meditation so refreshing and invigorating. Much more so than sleep.

Relaxation, of body and or of mind, is a decrease in *work*, a letting go of effort, a movement toward just being. But we keep talking about relaxing as something we *do*; as something we can learn *how* to do. Doesn't that mean there's some effort necessary in order to relax? Try the thing with your fist again. Certainly there's effort when you constrict the muscles. You intend to do it, and you make the effort. There's work involved. But the relaxation phase is a little different. You still intend to do it, but does it really require effort? I don't think so. What happens when you relax the muscles is that you take *away* the effort. You *allow* the muscles to return to a *natural state*. Relaxation is *allowing*, but it's done with intent.

Our confusion, if there is any, comes from the fact that we associate intent with effort. If we think about *doing* something, we assume it's going to take effort no matter what it is. So we say, "I'm trying to relax," and we can work very hard at trying to relax. Or we can work very hard at letting ourselves be. Like trying hard to be yourself. Or working at being spontaneous. And so forth. The grubby hands creeping in again. It's just very difficult for most of us to understand that we could be anything or do anything without putting a lot of effort into it.

Relaxation really means *no* effort. And if meditation means relaxed awareness, letting your mind be, getting your grubby hands off—then that means *no* effort too. Very few of us can just sit down and stop making effort. If we try, we'll find ourselves working hard at trying not to try.

That's where it really helps to learn how to let the body relax. We learn how to withdraw the effort and let the body go into its natural state. Then we move to let mind do the same. It is possible to *intend* to relax, but it is not possible to relax *effortfully*. Sometimes it takes a little nudge—a little

reminder—the slightest amount of effort—to begin the
relaxation process. But the process itself is one of taking
effort away; letting it go, letting things get natural. Like a
sigh.

Stretching   Physically, we often *stretch* in order to relax. After a
grueling day we may stretch widely and deeply before sitting
down to relax. There is nothing psychologically
sophisticated about stretching. Dogs and cats do a lot of it.
It's a way of *feeling* the muscles and getting them squared
away so we can let them go. It tells us where our muscles
are, so we can let them get back into a natural state.
Stretching is one of the very best ways to relax. You *do*
something that requires effort, and then you let go. Before
meditation, it is very helpful to do some stretching. Hatha
Yoga, which is in fact a very sophisticated and elaborate
arrangement of stretches, is ideally suited to this. It was
made for the purpose of getting the body ready, so that the
mind can get ready, for meditation.

If you look for them, you can find stretches all over the
place. The example I gave of clenching your fist and relaxing
it is a stretch. A yawn is a stretch for the muscles of jaw,
throat and chest. A deep breath is a stretch. You stretch on
the inbreath and relax on the outbreath. A sigh is a stretch.
There are stretches of the mind, too. As a matter of fact,
most of the specific forms of meditation—the things that are
done in meditation—are mental stretches. If you concentrate
on something, that's a stretch. It gets you aware of where
your mental "muscles" are or where the effort is going, so
that you can relax. If you chant the same sound over and
over again, it does the same thing. You bring effort to this,
and then you let go. The silence after the sound is the
relaxation. If you actively pray, that's a stretch. Then you
stop and listen, that's relaxation. *All the meditation methods
are ways of allowing your mind to relax, so it can go back,
like a muscle, to its natural state.*

This implies that most of the time our minds are in an
*un*natural state. I think that's true. Just like most of the time
our muscles are tense. Which is not their "natural" state.
This doesn't mean that muscles and minds should never get
tense—of course it is necessary that they contract and work
and produce effort. Otherwise the only things we'd be good
for would be paperweights or doorstops.

There's nothing bad or wrong about mental or muscular
tension. The problem is when our awareness gets caught in
that tension. If you had happened to have a butterfly in your
hand when you did the fist clenching exercise, it wouldn't
have done too well. It would get caught and squeezed and
lost and killed in the midst of the tightening muscles. The
same thing often happens to awareness in the midst of
mental tension. Fortunately, awareness is more resilient than
a butterfly. Because when the tension's over; when a pause
happens, or when we relax after a stretch, there it is! Alive
and well. Until it gets caught again.

Try it—right now take a deep inbreath and stretch.
Then exhale and relax everything. Let the muscles go. Let the

mind go. Do you sense the awareness flying free for just a moment?

That's why relaxation is important for meditation. You relax the body in order to relax the mind. You relax the mind in order to liberate awareness.

How you relax physically is not as important as *that* you relax. If you don't already know some Hatha Yoga asanas and breathing exercises, get a book on them or take a course. In the meantime, or maybe instead, begin with a deep inhale and big long standing-up drawn out stretch. Think of how Paul Bunyan would have stretched after waking up in the north woods on a bright spring morning. Big and emphatic and definite. Then as you exhale relax, think about letting go, about letting things get back to *natural,* and watch your mind get quieter. Lie down on your back and feel all the body settling down. Stretch again while you're lying down. Breath deeply, with gusto, using every cubic inch of air-space in your chest and stomach. Feel energy, brightness, alertness as you breathe in, and feel relaxation as you breathe out.

After a few breaths, lie very still for a while. Pay attention to your body and its muscles. Don't worry about awareness or mind yet—just get the body moving toward natural relaxation.

You can go over every muscle group in the body as you did with your fist—tensing and relaxing, if you wish. Just start at one end and work toward the other. These are the areas to include: toes, balls of feet, heels, ankles, shins and calves, knees, thighs (front, sides, back), buttocks, lower abdomen, sides, chest, lower back, upper back, shoulders, upper arms, elbows, forearms, wrists, hands, fingers, neck, jaw, cheeks, lips, nose, eyes, eyelids, eyebrows, forehead, scalp.

You should try this if you haven't already. Take your time with it, and don't move to another body area until the last is completely let go. Sense the relaxation as if it were flowing from one muscle group to the next. When you're finished, scan your body and let go of any places you still feel tension. Then just breathe for a while, getting wide awake and clear and energized with the inbreath, more and more relaxed with the outbreath. The state is one of total relaxation married to bright, clear alertness. No tension, nothing caught, no tightness anywhere. Whatever way you do it, give some real time before meditation to relaxing the body. It will make relaxation of the mind much easier.

I don't go through all the relaxation business *every* time I meditate. But that's only because I've learned that meditation *means* relaxation to me. When I sit down and get quiet, I feel all my muscles just letting go. They've learned— or I've learned—that that's just a part of meditating. But sometimes I still go through an extensive 10 - 30 minute routine of relaxation prior to meditation. Sometimes I need to. Sometimes I don't. The same will probably be true for you.

When you sit down to meditate, and you're all relaxed

and comfortable, see if you can just gently and effortlessly turn that same letting go process to the mind. If you can, and can let it stay relaxed, *letting it be* without any manipulation, then you've got what I consider the very best meditation and you ought to just stay with that. No fancy techniques are necessary.

After meditation

Relaxing after meditation is just as important as relaxing before. Because no matter how much we tell ourselves to let go, just be, relax, take it easy, allow, don't struggle, we still struggle. It's crazy how we set everything up to be comfortable and relaxed, so we can just be, and then we start trying to just be. In the meditation groups with which I work, the leader usually ends the silence by clapping his or her hands together quietly a couple of times. Then we just stretch out and kind of feel where we're at. Some of us write down a few notes about the experience. Then we discuss a little bit. It's not at all uncommon for somebody to say, "I just couldn't seem to get quiet. All through the silence I found myself struggling and trying. Then, when you clapped your hands and the meditation was over, *then* I relaxed and got quiet." This crazy thing happens so often that sometimes we take a very long time after the meditation is over, and sometimes that's when people really get quiet. Remember that when you're meditating. If it seems like a struggle, it might be worthwhile to just quit meditating. Then you'll be meditating.

Another value of the stretch-relax time after meditation is that it helps ease the transition between "meditative consciousness" and "normal consciousness," whatever that is. Ideally there should be no difference. But in terms of practical application, there does seem to be a difference. And if you jump right out of meditation into your usual management business, you can give your whole nervous system a shock it doesn't need. Take it very slowly and easily. Make all your transitions loosely, gently and fluidly. No jumping and jerking and shocking yourself.

Breathing

"And 'tis my faith, that every flower
Enjoys the air it breathes."
William Wordsworth, *Lines Written
in Early Spring*

Breathing is a very important part of almost every awareness-freeing tradition. Even the word "spirit" is part of "inspiration," "expiration," and "respiration."

I think the best thing about breathing (aside from the fact that it keeps you alive) is that it is just about the clearest example we have of how we can't be aware of something without getting our grubby hands on it. As in the example before when we tried to be aware of breathing without influencing it. This means breathing is an excellent thing to work with when we try to learn how to walk that difficult line between awareness and control. When a person learns how to watch his or her breathing without influencing it in the slightest, he or she will be very close to being able to do the same thing with the mind. Because of course, the mind is the same way. It runs along "by itself" when we're not paying attention to it, but it gets all glued up when we're watching.

Work with the breathing can constitute the sole practice of meditation. Some Zen groups do nothing but count the breaths, from one to three or one to ten, over and over again. Some Hinayana Buddhists just watch the stomach rising and falling, or feel the "touch" of the breath in the nostrils as it goes in and out. That's all. The middle-Eastern Hesychasts set the Jesus prayer to go with the breathing, and that was their very simple, silent way of prayer and meditation. On the inbreath it would be "Lord Jesus Christ," and on the outbreath "Have mercy upon me." So that after a while there was nothing but the prayer, going on and on by itself. When it got that deep, it became the "Prayer of the Heart," just going on and on. Some of those desert fathers would watch their stomachs going up and down with the breath and the prayer, much like the Hinayana Buddhists. Rumor has it that that's where the phrase "contemplating your navel" came from.

The other thing about breathing is that it's a great help in relaxing, as we discussed in the last section. A good deep inspiration and exhalation is just normally what we do to relax. When you are getting ready to sit down to meditate formally, it's best just to pay attention to your breathing and how it helps you relax. If you can do it this simple, gentle way, that's best. If it doesn't come that easy, then go ahead and do something special with the breathing, like deep slow breaths with relaxation increasing each time you exhale.

There are some traditions which make a very big deal

out of the breathing. Kundalini Yoga, for example, sees the breath as the way in which cosmic energy is carried into and out of the body through a series of channels and psychic clearing houses called chakras. Everybody says you shouldn't fool around with Kundalini without very competent guidance, and I guess that's true. I do know you can get yourself very hyperventilated and flaky when you're working with breathing and you don't know what you're doing.

Hyperventilation

Hyperventilation is a medical term which means that you've done a lot more breathing than your body needs. Each time you inhale, oxygen goes into your blood, and each time you exhale, carbon dioxide comes out. These two gases need to be in a kind of balance in the bloodstream as they influence both the acidity of the blood and certain centers in the brain which affect other body activities. What happens when you hyperventilate is that this balance gets out of whack and you begin to feel lightheaded and dizzy. There's a kind of buzzing sensation throughout the body. Then your fingers and toes start getting prickly and maybe you feel that same numb "pins and needles" sensation around your lips. If it keeps up long enough, you pass out. Then your breathing slows down until the oxygen/carbon dioxide balance gets back in order and then you wake up again. If what you're after is simply altering consciousness, that's sure one way to do it. And in that regard, it's probably a lot safer than using drugs or chemicals. But I hope what you're after is to *quit* altering consciousness, and let it be as clear and free and natural as possible.

The reason I'm going into this in such detail is so you'll know what's happening if you experience some of these sensations when you're working with your breathing. Some people hyperventilate when they get anxious, and the weird sensations of hyperventilation make them more scared, so they hyperventilate more, and it can produce a real panicky state. You can also get palpitations or a whopper of a headache from hyperventilation. If you do begin to feel dizzy when you're breathing deeply, there's nothing to worry about. Just slow your breathing down, or breathe more shallowly, or stop breathing altogether for a little while. Then the gas balance will adjust itself and you'll feel all right again.

Breathing practice

If you need to *do* something with your breathing beyond just paying attention to it or taking a few deep breaths, begin by lying very still on your back and breathing only with your stomach. As you breathe in, your stomach rises toward the ceiling. You can rest your hands on your stomach to feel this better. As you breathe out, your stomach falls back toward the floor. You notice that as you breathe in, your stomach muscles relax, letting go to make room for the incoming air. That's the way we naturally breathe. We don't *pull* the air in. We simply make space for it and the atmospheric pressure pushes it in to us. It just flows in and fills the space. Then when we breathe out, our stomach muscles contract to push all the air out. Contract them fully (without straining) to get all the air out. Just do that for a while. In this part of the exercise, your chest does not move at all. Stomach breathing like this is the way small children breathe, and how we often breathe when we're asleep. When we're not looking. When we're just acting natural. But when we're busily involved in our noisy lives, the breath is usually shallow, up high in the chest, with the abdominal muscles tight most of the time.

The stomach-breathing may be enough to help you get relaxed. If more is needed, make the breath more complete by using the chest as well as the stomach. When you breathe in, fill the stomach just as you did before. Only this time, when the stomach is full, go ahead and expand the chest to fill that as well. You take in more air this way. When you breathe out, contract the chest first, leaving the stomach sticking out until the chest seems empty. Then go ahead and contract the stomach, getting every last bit of air out. It's amazing how much air goes into one breath this way, compared to usual daily breaths which are as shallow as tissue paper. You should make this breathing sequence as smooth and flowing as possible. No strain, no jerking, no choppiness. Let one movement flow easily into the next. It takes some practice. Just work with the stomach first until you get it good and easy. Then move on to adding the chest. It's easy to remember the sequence of the breathing if you think of filling your lungs with air just as you fill a glass with water. The bottom (stomach) fills up first, then the top (chest). When you exhale, it's like pouring water out of a glass. The top empties first, then the bottom. When you get it right, it will be just as flowing and smooth as pouring water. Some of the specific meditation approaches we'll talk about include more work with the breathing, but this is probably enough to help get you relaxed before meditation.

Breathing yourself to sleep

I will add, as a real aside, that you can combine all this business of muscular relaxation and breathing to help you get to sleep at night if you have insomnia. You go through the muscular relaxation sequence, only this time rather than feeling your awareness get bright and clear, you go ahead and cloud it a little by the concentration on your muscles. When the muscles are relaxed, you start the complete in-out breathing process, again letting your awareness get cloudy rather than clear. Finally, you get a hold of your pulse, in your wrist. (Or if you're quiet enough you can just feel your heart beating inside you and use that.) Count the beats, and find a rhythm which is comfortable to breathe with. For example, breathe in for eight, hold for four, breathe out for eight, hold for four, breathe in for eight, etc. Or it may be seven and three, or five and two . . . you have to find the rhythm which is comfortable. Whatever you settle on, it should be the same number of heartbeats for the inbreath and outbreath, and about half that number for each hold. You're a pretty good insomniac if you can stay awake with all this.

I hope you noticed a bad aroma surrounding this technique. I've just given you a way to manipulate your consciousness. Which is precisely what this book is about *not* doing. If you're trying to go to sleep and you can't, it means that you have decided somewhere that you *should* go to sleep and you've engaged your mind in a battle about it. Your awareness has been trapped in the process. It would be *much* more healthy for your awareness if you just said to your mind, "Here we are lying in this bed at three o'clock in the morning, and I'm wanting to get to sleep because I've got a busy day tomorrow. But you don't want to sleep, mind of mine, and that's your prerogative. If that's the way you want it, O.K. We'll just lie here together and you can jump around all you want until *you're* ready to sleep. I don't care if it takes forever. I'll survive. Go ahead. I'm just going to lie here and watch."

What this does is pull one side out of the battle. A unilateral withdrawal. And when there's nobody left to fight with, the struggle stops. And your awareness is set free. Then you just might find you go to sleep. Or you may stay awake. If you do, you're using the time to meditate, and tomorrow, during the time you were going to meditate, you can take a nap.

I presented that going-to-sleep method because it works, and because I know that though we can *cultivate* the recommended letting-be attitude toward our minds, we can't expect ourselves to pull it off every time. Or even most of the time. I figure if we *must* struggle with ourselves, which we must, we might as well accept that and do it quickly and effectively rather than dragging it out and making a big deal of it. The ultimate awareness, or at least one closer to the ideal, would be to see ourselves struggling with ourselves, getting our grubby hands all over ourselves, and to *watch* it, without any comment or intervention at all. That's the penultimate non-manipulation. Then you're not even struggling not to struggle. You're not trying not to try. There's all sorts of activity and hi-jinks going on, and you're just in there sensing it all. That's beautiful. The ultimate, of course, is just to be brightly aware, with no separate watching going on.

Remember that business about trying and struggling if you can. Because when we sit down to meditate we'll find ourselves trying to do something. Trying to relax. Trying to let ourselves be. Trying to keep our grubby hands off. Trying to get quiet. Always, always trying. Most of the time we just work with that the best we can. But now and then, on rare occasions at the beginning, we find that we can just watch it *all* going on and *let* it all go on. That, as far as I'm concerned, is very good. Let your mind be. Let your impulses be. Let your conscience be. Let the struggles between your conscience and your impulses be. And even let your letting be be. Ultimate permissiveness. Total acceptance, not choosing one side or another. When that happens, you're even beginning to cease watching it. Brightly aware, but ceasing to watch, because there's no separate part of you that's watching. You are dissolved in it and it doesn't matter

where your sense of "me" is. What matters is that awareness
is free and clear, and you are at one with your living. Just
being. Fully and completely. Totally involved, clean, pure
and unfettered.

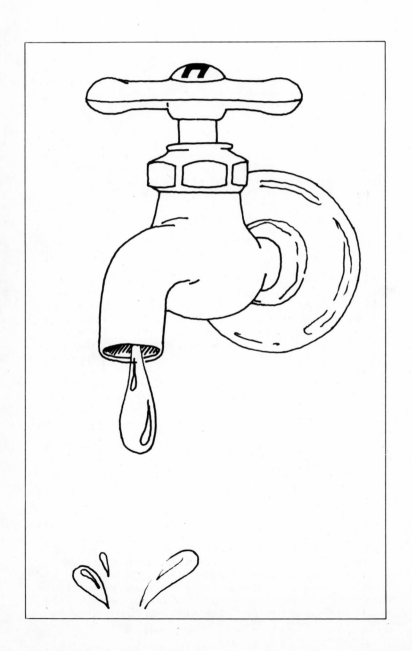

Handling "Distractions"

"It will be generally admitted that Beethoven's Fifth
Symphony is the most sublime noise that has ever
penetrated into the ear of man."
Edward Morgan Forster,
Howards End

Distraction and desire
You notice that I often put "distractions" in quotation
marks. That's because there really is no such thing.
"Distractions" occur only if we're trying to focus on one
thing and shut others out. If you're really open to what is,
there is no such thing as a distraction. Distractions are like
noises. A noise is a sound we don't want. A symphony can
be noise if it's playing in the background when we're trying
to concentrate on something else. The laughter of children
playing can be exquisite beauty or ultimate awfulness.
Distractions are also like weeds. A weed is an unwanted
plant. A beautiful daffodil can be a weed if it's growing in
our orchid patch. It all depends on our attitude, which is
determined by our desire. Desire defines what will be a
noise, a weed or a distraction.

Sources
Distractions will seem to occur from all fronts. They'll
come from your environment in the form of noises,
temperature changes, and movement. They'll come from
your body in the form of itches, pains, stomach grumbles,
belches, sneezes, throat tickles, palpitations, and countless
weird sensations like electrical vibrations or water running
over your head or your skin crawling. They'll come from
your mind in a myriad of ways. Splashing colors in your
eyeballs, voices speaking in your ears, psychic experiences,
vivid memories, constant thoughts of what you should be
doing instead of meditating, sexual fantasies, all sorts of
emotions, and crazy feelings like leaving your body or
feeling very light or heavy or hot or cold. There is no end to
them. What we need to work toward is letting them be there,
letting them come and go, letting them come into our
awareness without getting hooked by them. No matter how
enticing, seductive, entertaining, important, mystical,
religious, powerful, demonic, satanic, sacred or terrorizing
they seem, just let them be. If you have any reaction to them,
it should be no more than "hmmm." No matter what!

Usual handling
Our usual way of handling distractions is to kill our
awareness of them. Recently I was in a room, involved in an
intense conversation with some colleagues. Over in the
corner was an old fan that was rattling and chattering and
acting as if it were about to take off. But we hardly even
heard it. Those of us who did hear it felt a moment's
frustration with it, then would tune it out and go back to the
conversation. It took *work* to keep up the conversation. We
had to strain to listen. The work went into shutting out the

noise of the fan. After the conversation many of us felt tired.
Some even had headaches. If some disgustingly sensible
person had asked "Why didn't you just turn it off?" we
might have answered: "We were too involved in the
conversation. It didn't seem worth it to interrupt our
discussion to turn it off." Instead of turning it off, we tuned
it out. But we didn't realize how much energy it took to tune
it out.

Free flowing   If we had *really* been into saving energy, we could have
just turned the fan off. *Or,* we might have been able to let
the fan continue its chatter, allowed it to come into our
consciousness and still have gone on about our business. We
didn't *have* to shut it out. It could have been in our
consciousness without disturbing us. *Just because something
comes into your consciousness doesn't mean you have to pay
attention to it.* You don't have to do *anything* with it. It can
go in one ear and out the other. In the eyeballs and right on
out through the back of the head. In with the inbreath, out
with the outbreath. It can flow right on through. Open
channel. Just because it's there doesn't mean you have to
catch it and mess with it. You can if you want to, but you
certainly don't have to. It is marvelous to discover that you
can have lots of things in your consciousness, fully and
clearly, and not pay attention to any of them. Or that you
can have nothing special at all in your consciousness, and
pay absolute attention. That's freedom of awareness.

Seeing everything   Try another experiment. Look around you, wherever
you are right now. See everything but pay attention to
nothing. Just let all the sights come in and go out. Let them
all enter your awareness but don't hang on to any of them.
Don't label or interpret them in any way. The first few
times, you'll hang up on a few things, and if you want to
analyze it you'll find they're somehow hooked up to your
desires. You also may find that in trying not to pay attention
to anything you tend to dull your vision. That's our habitual
tendency. But with a little practice you can get your eyes
open and clear enough so all the visual stimuli just come on
in. And go right on out again as you move your eyes.
Nothing gets held on to.

Paying attention   When you can do that fairly well, try picking one object
out of your surroundings and pay attention to it. Go ahead
and make it the center of your attention. But don't shut out
the *others.* Let them be fully in awareness while you're still
centered on your chosen object. That's even more difficult.
But you can do it.

In this kind of awareness, there can be no
"distractions." All the stimuli are in your consciousness;
you're allowing them, but you're still paying attention to
something else. This is a fine example of how you can
conserve energy by keeping awareness open and free, and
still go on about your business.

This is not *too* hard when you're sitting in a sort of
bland, uninteresting or unthreatening environment. But if a
nice sex object comes walking by, or someone frowns at you,
or something very "important" happens, then it becomes

much more difficult. Then you get a clear sense of how entrenched your consciousness-killing habits are. And how they're hooked on desire.

Letting distractions come and go

All of this points in the direction of how we should deal with "distractions" in meditation. There should be none. But nothing should be tuned out either. Any sound, image, thought, noise, stimulus or whatever that occurs should just be allowed. You don't have to pay attention, but you don't have to shut it out either. Let them all come in. Act as though you're going to be a gracious host. "Y'all come on in. You all are welcome." Just don't get involved with entertaining your guests. Let them come in through the front door and pass out the back.

This is the ideal of how distractions are handled. But in practical terms, we have to recognize that our habits are strong and not easily changed. We will find ourselves paying attention to many stimuli, and letting our awareness get trapped by them. We have to allow that. Because to fight it will create more awareness-swallowing struggles. And we can't win anyway. Not right off.

Re-opening to awareness

So when we *do* get "distracted," when our consciousness *does* get carried off by this image or that worry or whatever, we just wait till the realization comes to us: "Ah, I got distracted." Then there should be no recriminations, no sense of "I'll have to try harder," no hassle. You just open up again. Relax a little more. Maybe start watching again. No problem. If your attention doesn't want to come back quite yet, be permissive. Wait until it's ready.

And remember that there's something very valuable about "distractions." When your consciousness seems to have been "off" somewhere for a while, kidnapped by something, you have a chance to sense it coming home. And it's in that moment, between recognizing you've been "distracted" and the reopening of awareness, that you get to sense awareness most intimately. That's when you really feel it. In that little time it takes just to gently make it free, you begin to make friends with it. You can't hold it, but you can sort of stroke its feathers as it comes by. Of course, there's still a separate "you" in there somewhere, but it's close. And very beautiful.

The cat

Don't expect yourself to be able to adopt this easy-open-channel approach to distractions right away. Let yourself get sidetracked just as often as it happens. With some time, you'll sense that the free awareness is lasting longer and longer. You can't force it. Distractions are all determined by our desire, which brings in control, which brings in all the management struggle. Just let it be, management and all. Don't expect too much of yourself.

I remember when Betty, my wife, was learning TM. She was sitting there one day, "trying to meditate," when our youngest son matter-of-factly came in and dumped our cat squarely on top of her head. This was a distraction. She asked our teacher what to do about that kind of distraction. In fine TM form he said, "Just go back to the mantra." "But

there was a *cat* on my *head!* The instructor went on to
explain how he'd learned to meditate next to dynamite blasts.
Betty was fairly yelling at this point. "You see, there was a
CAT ON MY HEAD!" Well, she needed permission to be
distracted. After all, you're not going to be a Zen master
right off. As a matter of fact, I've had some fantasies about
what a Zen master would do if you dumped a cat on his head
while he's meditating. Bald head. There's an old Zen story
about a master cutting a cat in half to make a point, so I
wouldn't try it. But I wonder. My sneaking suspicion is that
he'd take the cat off his head, put it on the floor, maybe pet
it once, and then go back to his sitting. And none of it would
be a distraction. It would all be meditation.

The goal and the path   The point is that when we begin meditating, and probably for many years thereafter, we still have the habit of paying attention to something and shutting out other things. This means that we are going to feel as if we must do something about distractions. Maybe the ideal is for us to realize we can just open awareness and not have to shut anything out, but we're just not "there" yet. We must not confuse the goal with our place on the path. We have to allow and accept the fact that we will feel distracted whether we really are or not, and that we will feel we must *do* something with the stimuli that reach consciousness whether we really need to or not.

Chapter Fifteen

Effort

"Striving to better, oft we mar what's well."
William Shakespeare,
King Lear

Harmony　　Just as there is a difference between pain and suffering, there is a difference between energy and effort. Both pain and energy are free, vibrant dynamic forces which can be seen flowing openly in the process of life. In moments when one is in harmony with the true *unity* of being, there is no imposition or barricade to the flow of pain and energy.

Separation　　But it is part of humanity's given condition that we feel *separate* most of the time. Then we are bound to clench our teeth, wince, struggle and grapple with pain. This is called suffering. And we are bound to clench our fists, grimace, grunt and groan with energy. This is called effort.

Acceptance　　Until it is possible to be in the dynamic flow of energy and cease to define ourselves away from it, we must accept our need to make effort. In this light, it is possible to look at the different kinds of effort we make.

Efforts　　Effort can fuel the very fire of meditation, or it can be the water which puts out that fire. Which it will be depends in large part upon one's level of delicacy. There are two basic kinds of effort, and both have a role in meditation. For lack of a sophisticated terminology, I'll call them "regular effort" and "meditative effort."

Regular Effort

Forcing　　Regular effort is the kind which involves hard work. Pushing or pulling on something; applying a force against some resistance. This is the kind of effort which can ruin meditation, because it very easily becomes associated with a bulldozer approach. Where you want to achieve something and work hard to "get" it. In meditation, this will only leave you tired and bruised. But there are three occasions when regular effort is valuable in a meditative way.

Beginning　　One is at the beginning of meditation, when it takes a little nudge to get started. In the beginning, our minds are so used to making effort that they get very restless if they have nothing to work at. So you give your mind something simple to do. You let it make some effort. Like looking at something or listening to something or paying attention to something in particular. Then *as soon* as your mind gets comfortable with this, give up the effort altogether. Stop trying to meditate. No effort whatsover. Then will come another time when your mind starts needing something to do, so you let it go back and put some effort into paying attention. Until it becomes comfortable again.

xperimenting　　The second time regular effort is appropriate is when you need to *experiment*. Sometimes you need to feel what effort is like. You need to explore the nature and substance of work. It is good to make effort when you are trying to experience what exactly effort is, and what it does to your consciousness. The difference here, and this is important to remember, is that *in this kind of effort you are not trying to achieve anything.* If you make a lot of effort in trying to get quiet, or trying to clear your mind or trying to get spiritually developed or trying to get aware, you will defeat yourself. But if you make effort for the purpose of learning what effort is, for learning about your limits, for experiencing the relationship between effort and awareness, then there will be no problem. When you are experimenting with effort, you may want to push very hard, work to the point where you are truly fatigued. This is fine if you're not trying to get anything.

Preparing for relaxing

The third time regular effort can be good for meditation is as a *preparation for relaxation.* Sometimes when we want to relax the body, we tense it up first so we can feel where it is and what it's like. Then we can let it relax. Like a stretch. The same thing can be done with the mind. Sometimes you need to give the mind a bit of a stretch before you can let it relax. On occasion when I sit down to meditate, my mind seems kind of "stuck," sort of tight and rigid and rusty. It moves ponderously rather than smoothly and freely. This is especially true in the morning. It's as if it really has a lot of cobwebs in it after a night's sleep. Then I often find it helpful to put my mind through a little exercise before I meditate. Like reciting something silently to myself, trying to get the words clear and not drift off somewhere while I'm doing it. Sometimes I use a prayer, or a bit of poetry, or a visual image. Something to get the mind awake and working. Sometimes I *push* it then. But only for a little while. And only for the purpose of waking up and loosening up.

Meditative Effort

Effortless effort

This effort is one of the roughest paradoxes in meditation. What is the nature of the effort which takes incredible perseverance, supreme endurance, and yet no force whatsoever? How can one describe the effort of relaxation? The effort of gentleness? The effort of acceptance? It is in fact the effort of remaining effortless.

To be aware, free and clear right now, requires precisely the right amount of energy. Which is that equal to the force of a falling snowflake. Any less and one slips into a self-stifling dullness. Any more and one has hopped on a bulldozer and destroyed everything.

For a moment, now and then, this is easy. Immediate awareness is seen with simply the blink of an eye or a little sigh. But to *stay* aware; to *remain* in the midst of totally free awareness while mind and body and will all move in to trap it; this requires an incredibly fierce endurance. An endurance of delicacy.

To stay present and alive is to stand tip-toe on the knife edge of gentleness while all around are voices screaming "work at it," "try harder," "accomplish something." To simply stay there while identity dies a thousand deaths, ego writhes like a snake caught by a forked stick, and self-image rumbles like an earthquake beneath you; this is meditative effort.

I really need not attempt to describe it, for it is clear enough when experienced. All too clear. The effort of staying effortless is the true fire of meditation. The fire in which many dear possessions are consumed, yet also in which the bonds of awareness are burned through and being is set free.

No ownership

How colorful and dramatic I try to make this seem. You see how I have made it special. This is an old habit of mine; there always seems to be something very mystical about effortless effort. And there is always some tendency to expect miraculous things to come from it. I suppose that's because as one sees one's own personal power dying and dying again, one begins to hope for a transpersonal power to replace it. The trouble is that though the transpersonal power is very real, one simply can't appropriate it for one's self. All the power of the universe is there, but it cannot co-exist with personal identity. One can be dissolved within it, but never proclaim it as "mine."

The paradox

Nearly everyone who steps upon a path of prayer or meditation encounters this paradox. Repeated visions of mystical abilities occur. The trouble is, they *just happen.* Much as one might like, there is no way of taking credit for them. No way to make them one's own. Faith can indeed move mountains. But there's a catch. A very irritating catch. Seeing that a mountain has in fact been moved, there is no way under heaven that one can say "I did it."

On my better days, I have no fantasy of being able to "attain" some single-pointedness of mind so that I can possess fantastic power. But there are other days.

Moments

I guess it's part of being human, but there are still times when I'm sitting there and I get very impressed with the wonderfulness of my awareness and the stillness of my mind and I start thinking about all those stories I read about mystics in India who had such mental powers that they could move objects with their gaze or even levitate themselves right off the floor. And I begin to think, "Hmmmmm. Maybe. . . ." And I find myself working. I haven't any idea what earthly use there could be to having the ability to levitate oneself or make an object fly around the room with your mind. Its only purpose is one I don't like to admit. Show. It would make a neat performance. People might gather round and say, "Hey, look what Jerry can do!" And others would say, "It's a fake." And maybe I'd get to go on some late-night talk show and do my thing. Only then it wouldn't work because I'd be nervous and I wouldn't be able to concentrate. But still, just maybe. . . .

That's all a big trap. Ultimately, it's just a threatened self-image trying to re-establish its importance. Not too long ago, it caught me again. Maybe for the last time, though I wouldn't bet on it. I was sitting in the middle of the living room floor, meditating. It was very quiet and I'd been able to

Power

meditate for quite a while. It was all going superbly. One of
those really neat times when things click. Awareness was
like a flawless diamond. Perfect. My eyes fell on an object on
the floor about six feet away from me. It was the bottom of
a little humidifier that we use when our kids get colds. It was
about eight inches high and I could see, over the top, that
there was a little water left in it. I couldn't see the full surface
of the water, but what I did see was so still and calm and clear
that it reminded me of my own awareness. As I sat there
watching the still water, I remembered an exercise I'd once
done in which you float a needle on water and try to make it
turn by the force of your concentration. One of those hard-
push exercises. It had always left me with a headache,
irritable, and frustrated. And the needle had never moved.

I thought, "Yes, that hard-push way certainly was not
for me. This open, allowing way is so much better." But
then, like a dark cat sneaking up on its prey, another
thought crept around the deep corners of my mind. "You
know, it wouldn't take much force to cause a little ripple in
that water. Just to disturb the surface a little. Maybe you
could just try. Nothing spectacular. Just a little ripple on the
surface of that water." I succumbed. I was so clear, it
seemed, that if I could ever "do it," I could do it then. So I
started concentrating. "Remember," I told myself, "if you
try too hard, it won't happen." So I just hung out with the
water, nurturing the little thought that it would ripple. Very
sophisticated approach. Not to *try* to make it ripple, but to
center in on it and carry the idea that it *would* ripple.

Several minutes passed. Nothing happened. I found
myself trying harder. Pushing. Still nothing happened. I was
getting tired. Finally, I thought, "This is getting me
nowhere. I quit." Then, just as it happens in all the stories,
in that very instant, a little ripple went across the water. It
scared me. I wasn't even sure I'd seen it. Maybe I'd been
trying so hard I'd just imagined it. But it certainly stimulated
me to try again.

So I went back to concentrating. This time, though, I
was trying to give up. That's when it happens. When you
give up and let go of it. That's when the power comes
through. Or so I'd heard. So I was trying to give up.
Nothing happened. Finally, I got tired of trying to give up
and gave up. Ripple. I was sure I saw it that time. Try again.
Give up again. Ripple. Pretty soon I was excited and scared
and happy and confused and I decided it was time to stop,
let it all go, and get on with my business. As I got up, a little
thought came about wanting to tell somebody about it—to
brag just a little—but I decided not to. No sense making more
of an ego thing of it than it already was. In leaving, I glanced
down, rather affectionately, at the little pan of water.
Floating there, in the part of the water I couldn't see when
I'd been sitting, was a fly. It was in the final throes of a
drowning death. As I watched it, it moved one tiny leg. Just
a bit. Ripple.

Part III

Bases for Formal Meditation

"But such a tide as moving seems
        asleep,
    Too full for sound and foam,
When that which drew from out the
        boundless deep
    Turns again home."
Alfred Lord Tennyson, *Crossing the Bar*

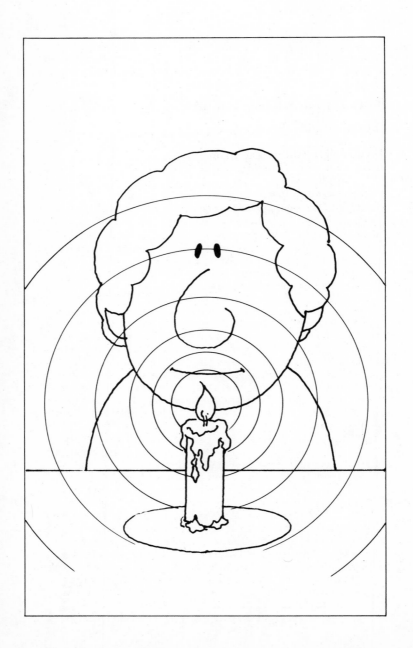

The Centering Process

"Center down."
A Quaker saying

A home   Centering is using a crutch. It is an aid in becoming immediately open to what is. It gives us some object, image or activity which acts as a home base for attention, a central pivotal point about which consciousness can move.

Three myths   There are three basic myths which we carry around inside us and use to help keep our self-image strong and our awareness trapped:

1. When we are aware, we feel we must focus that awareness *on* something.
2. We feel we must shut out everything we don't need to pay attention to.
3. We feel we must *do* something about everything of which we are aware.

Three truths   To realize that these assumptions are basically false is not enough. The habit is too great, and it is impossible to rip these beliefs off and have done with them. No amount of rational explanation will eradicate these habits. The only way is to discover, through practice, little by little, that:

1. We don't *have* to focus on anything.
2. We don't *have* to shut anything out.
3. We don't *have* to manipulate awareness in any way.

Three gifts   Our minds would become very anxious if we tried to divest them of these habits abruptly, so the process of centering is what we use to allow the process to occur more gradually, at the rate which is right for our own individual minds. The centering process allows us to continue the awareness-trapping habits in less and less dramatic ways:

1. Centering gives us something upon which to focus attention. Something simple which doesn't take much effort, and which can be relinquished easily when we're ready.
2. It allows us to shut out *some* stimuli, but gently prepares us to feel comfortable with letting other stimuli come in. More and more.
3. Finally, centering gives us something simple to *do* with whatever is in awareness. Something increasingly simple.

A base   The essence of centering is to provide a base for attention. This base, or central focus, can be anything. Breathing, a candle flame, a flower, body movement, sound, anything. Whatever it is, all one does is simply pay attention to it. Be interested in it. Then, when thoughts drift away and awareness becomes trapped somewhere "off" and out of the immediate moment, one simply comes back to the base. Come home.

It is very important (grin) to remember that paying

attention to the base is not the goal of meditation. There is nothing special or great about being able to sit there with the base totally centered in your mind and to have no distractions. The paying attention is a crutch. We only do it because we have to, and hopefully for no longer than we have to.

Take a specific example. Say that the base is to be a **An example** candle flame. Good old standard meditation object which has been used in a multitude of spiritual traditions. With a candle, the centering process is as follows:

1. Get your time and place set up, comfortable and *relatively* free of distractions.
2. Light the candle. No ceremony necessary. No ceremony unnecessary.
3. Do some of the breathing-relaxation stuff.
4. Take some time to get your position into one that feels good. Make it a comfortable distance from the candle, so that *no* eye effort is needed. Not so close that it's too bright, nor so far that you need to strain to see it.
5. Relax some more and breathe some more.
6. Look at the candle. *Don't* stare. Don't try to avoid blinking. Just look at it. Watch it. Comfortably. Be open to the tension between your eyebrows or in your forehead. If any occurs, let it relax and smooth out.
7. Now here's the tricky part. You can say that you're *concentrating* on the candle, but be sure you understand what that means. It does mean that your attention begins upon the candle and returns to it from time to time. It does *not* mean that you try to keep anything else from coming into your mind. Anything that wants to come in, ANYTHING, you just let it come. Whatever comes in, just be very loose with it. You don't need to hold it or push on it or do anything with it. If you *do* feel the need to mess with something, that's what the candle is for. If you must pay attention to something, pay attention to the candle. Otherwise, just watch everything coming and going. Nothing more.
8. With this process going on, there really is nothing which is a distraction. Everything just comes and goes. But there will be plenty of times when you *feel* distracted. When your awareness becomes kidnapped by something, and you lose touch with the open present watching. That's fine. That's perfect! No struggle. That's when you simply and *gently* come home to the candle. No extra effort. The force of a snowflake. The very gentlest of nudges. If there is some resistance, and attention doesn't seem to want to come back to the candle, don't fight. Just say "O.K." and wait. Practice waiting. Very patient and very permissive.

9. Once the process is underway, quit trying! Just let it
happen. Just be. Stop trying to meditate. Stop
trying to do anything. A master put it very
succinctly to me when I was having trouble with
meditation. He said, "As soon as you sit down to
meditate, quit meditating. Quit it entirely." At first
this didn't make sense, because I was still very
glued to the idea that meditation is something one
does. But in practice, it "worked." As soon as I
really quit, meditation happened.

10. If you find yourself trying, quit. If you find yourself
trying to keep from trying, quit that. Finally, as in
the old Zen saying, quit quitting. Just keep quitting
until you're finally relaxed and open with all that is
going on in your mind, and with all that is going
on around you.

These ten steps are a rather complete description of
working with a base. Don't expect to "make" it to the point
of really quitting quitting at all. Sometimes it might happen
to you, but just accept whatever is going on with your
meditation, whether it seems "successful" or not.

The becomings After a while, things may become very quiet. It may be a
long while, or it may be a short while. In many meditations,
it won't happen at all. But sometimes things will become
awesomely quiet. It will seem like there is nothing at all in
consciousness, but you are somehow still aware. This is fine.
It's part of freeing awareness, and it's very refreshing, and
sometimes a bit scary. But don't make a big deal out of it.
Some people call it samadhi, or consciousness without
content, or cosmic or transcendental consciousness. Other
very respected traditions call it inertia. Don't get hung up
with what it is or with trying to keep it. It won't stay if you
try to keep it anyway. Just handle it like everything else. Let
it be. If you find any trying going on about it, that's when to
get back to the base. There are all sorts of "new" kinds of
consciousness-experiences which occur with meditation.
Don't go chasing after any of them. Don't go running away
either. Handle them like any other stimulus. Some are pure
and crystal clear. Others are exciting and fascinating. Some
are absolute perceptions of what is. Others are figments of
your own mind, trying to get you caught up and led astray.
And you don't know which is which. So don't pay any
special attention to any of them. Come back home, to the
base.

Figuring out This problem of figuring out what's pure and what isn't
crops up again and again in spiritual traditions. In the
depths of prayer or meditation, something occurs which
seems very profound. What is it? Where does it come
from? St. John of the Cross experienced the same dilemma.
"Is it the voice of God or of Satan?" he would ask. His
suggestion about this problem is to pay no attention to it. No
matter where it may come from. If it comes from Satan, he
says, you certainly don't want to pay attention to it. If it
comes from God, it will show up in other ways later. So just
go back to the base.

Come back That's what the base is for. To come back to whenever you find yourself trying, struggling, working, etc. A colleague of mine gave this description: "The base is like one of those pilings on a dock that boats tie up to. It's as if I'm at sea, floating on the waves of thoughts and images, and all the time, I'm gently tethered to the piling. I may drift off on the waves, and temporarily lose sight of the piling, but never for too far or for too long. Pretty soon, the rope draws up, and I see where I am. It's like being able to ride the waves of consciousness without fear of getting lost."

Another person described the base as "a little light, a guide I follow in darkness. I'm just following it, and though I stray from its path again and again, all I have to do is look around, and I see it there. I need not follow it closely. It's always there."

Pro and con The centering process has both assets and liabilities in the light of the larger process of letting yourself be who you most naturally and vibrantly are. Centering helps by giving you something simple to do with your addiction-to-doing, and this makes it possible to relax. But centering can also kill your relaxation if you make work of it. It can help you remain openly aware by giving you something right here and now to pay attention to, but it can just as easily kill your awareness if you start concentrating on the base and shutting other things out. So again it is a matter of keeping a delicate balance. An equilibrium which is incredibly simple but not at all easy.

From attention to being At the beginning, the "center" of the centering process is the object of meditation—whatever object or activity you choose to be the base for attention. Later on, as some of the awareness-trapping habits loosen a bit around the edges, it will be less and less necessary for you to home in on something. Then it seems that the center is becoming larger, expanding to include more and more of you and your environment. As this happens, distinctions between "me and it" become less rigid. Eventually, perhaps, the center is everywhere, because you're not shutting anything out and you're not struggling with anything. When does this happen? It happens in little moments all the time. But I don't know when it happens permanently. Maybe not in this lifetime. Maybe never. Maybe this evening. One never knows. That's the way we are.

The goal and the path Just don't get hung up with trying to "make" it happen. It is nothing to be achieved. Don't confuse your frozen image of the goal with the beautiful fluid reality of the path you're traveling right now. Just appreciate the little expansions you begin to notice. The flower of awareness is growing. Its petals are unfolding. Appreciate that process, and rejoice as it weathers storms and dry spells. Don't try to make the flower grow faster. Don't pull on the petals. Look closely and see that it is exquisitely perfect, just as it is, growing, opening, unfolding.

Choosing a Method

"We never do anything well till we cease to think about the manner of doing it."
William Hazlitt,
Sketches and Essays

Sources   The different kinds of meditation which follow are determined simply by what is used as a base for attention. You can see by glancing over them that nearly anything can be used as a base, and at the beginning it may seem difficult to make a choice. All of the bases and methods herein have been valuable to other people. Some of them are pieces of ancient spiritual traditions, while others are relatively "new." Some are simple, some complex.

Don't feel you have to follow any special order or curriculum with them, and certainly don't feel you must experiment with them all. I have included such a wide variety because people have different tastes and needs, and because I am firmly convinced that there is no one "right" way for people to enter formal meditative practice. Some people find body movement easier than sound. Others feel better with visual activity. Still others feel more comfortable with mind-things. Look all the approaches over, listen to yourself, and do what seems right. Experiment a little, but don't make a big serious heavy thing of it. If you do, everything will start to become important and you will start to feel very important too. And then you will have more trouble than ever just being. How could anyone who is *so important* just be?

Criteria   When you're trying to select a method, take three things into consideration:

1. The approach you choose should feel "right."
2. You should feel comfortable with it.
3. Given the above, the simpler the method, the better.

Natural   I don't know how to describe what feeling "right" is. As with so many other things in awareness, it just doesn't go into words well. Feeling right does not mean sensing something you "should" or "ought to" do. It means more a kind of feeling like "Oh, yes, this is for me." It feels natural rather than contrived. It feels like something you could easily fall into. It seems sort of like "home." It really is both an intuitive feeling and a rational conclusion. When something feels good intuitively but seems wrong to your sense of reason, or vice versa, you have conflict. But if something feels good intuitively and also fits with your rational understanding, your mind sort of clicks and you sense, "Yes, this is right." That's what I mean.

Comfortable   There seems to be very little constancy in the human mind about what feels right, or about what seems comfortable. This means you should leave plenty of room for flexibility in your approach. One day it might be best to lean back, relax, and do a very gentle, non-demanding meditation. The next, it may seem more comfortable to be much more rigorous and disciplined. The day after that, it may seem right not to meditate formally at all. This is a tricky business. On the one hand, you don't want to be so rigid that you wind up just going through the motions of some procedure simply because that's what you decided to do. On the other hand, you don't want to go frittering your time away trying one approach after another and not going into any of them in depth. There are traditions which prescribe one method and say "This is what you do, whether you want to or not, nothing more, nothing less, till you see it all the way through." There are other approaches (which can't be called traditions because there's nothing of substance to last from one generation to the next) which say "Whatever you feel like doing, do it. Follow your whims."

Simple   You need to be somewhere in between these two extremes; someplace where you are conscious of the need for constancy and depth, but where you are also free enough to change your tactics when you need to. Again, this requires an integrated use of both intuition and reason.

Keeping this in mind, finding a method which is comfortable simply means that the degree of effort and intent necessary for the method not be so great that the practice itself is disturbed. You maybe have to put *some* effort out at the beginning, just a little nudge, in order to meditate. But if you put out too much effort you'll find yourself trying to meditate instead of meditating. Trying to be instead of being.

If by chance there are several methods which feel right and comfortable, choose the simplest. As I've said before, our minds are so used to lots of activity and noise in the beginning that we may need a fairly complex method. Our minds might get anxious without a lot to "do." But as we get simpler and simpler techniques. Graduate to simplicity. The simplest forms of meditation are clearly the best, because there's little or no distance between them and your daily life. Which means it doesn't take much for the experience of life to be the experience of meditation and vice versa. Which further means awareness is very nearly free. Sometimes we get the idea that free awareness is something very complicated to be achieved. This leads us to expect that highly complex methods and great effort are needed. But that whole idea is fallacious. Free awareness is not something very complicated, to be achieved. It is something very simple, to be allowed.

Techniques   There is another thing you should watch out for in selecting a method. One of the problems with presenting a variety of techniques like this is that your mischievous mind will avoid getting quiet by trying one technique after another and telling you all the time, "Well that one is not getting me quiet, maybe this one will." A whole lot of noise can be generated that way. That's why I really like the simplicity of certain traditions, like Zen, which say, "Count your breaths, that this book contains, you'll just have to recognize it when it happens. It might help to tell your mind, "Now for this period of meditation, we're going to do this thing and that's all." That's if your mind behaves itself. It may tell you to bug off and head off on its own. You have to be a very gentle, understanding parent to your mind. If it gets rebellious you just smile in an understanding, condescending way. "O.K., little mind, off you go. Go ahead and do your thing. Both you and I know that it's just plain dumb, but there's no sense in arguing. You have to learn. You'll be back." When your mind wants to run away from home, help it pack its knapsack. Then wait at the door till it comes back. It will. But as much as possible, try to select your method before meditation, not during. Don't get into the habit of switching horses in mid-meditation any more than is necessary.

Practice   Perhaps these ideas will help in your selection of methods, but you will have to use some trial and error as well. If you're ambivalent about a method—if it seems to hold some promise but you're just not sure—then spend some time with it. Practice it for at least a week or two to see how it grows or doesn't grow on you.

One approach   While it's best to stick with one approach for a while and experience it in depth, this does not mean you have to use the specific methods described in this section. They are really just suggestions to get you started. You can combine parts of different suggestions into *one* approach for yourself. For example, you could combine a chant or silent mantra with a visual image. Or combine sound with body movement. Remember that one method is not inherently better or worse than another. It's your own internal experience, and the simplicity of that experience, which counts. Don't struggle to become "adept" at some method just because it sounds sophisticated. One person I know struggled for months to keep the image of a cross constantly in her mind during the entire meditation period. Finally, she achieved it. She announced with great pride that she had sat absolutely still for thirty minutes and the image had never wavered. Then, in a much softer voice, she added, "It certainly was boring."

Chances are, the most mediocre-sounding methods will be the best, because you don't have to worry so much about their becoming special. After all, it's not the method which is important. It's the wide-awake naturalness of your being.

With all the bases, use the following sequence:

Sequence
1. Select your time and place.
2. Stretch and relax the body. Take time enough to do this completely.
3. Pay attention to your breathing.
4. Find a comfortable relaxed/alert position.
5. Start out paying attention to the object or activity which you've chosen. Just the tiniest bit of effort here.

6. Then let your mind be. No effort. Stop trying to meditate.
7. Come back to the base whenever you need to; when there's a struggle or when you've been "off" somewhere.
8. Whenever you can let go of any part of the meditative process and stay clear, do so. Whenever you can become more simple, or move back closer to the basic practice, do so.
9. When you've finished, stretch, relax again, and let your consciousness flow into informal meditation for the rest of the day.

Whatever technique or method you choose, *give yourself to it* during the meditation. This means that you decide how you're going to start, do it, and then *give over* to it. Let it carry you, guide you, embrace you. Relax and be within it.

With Breathing or Sound as Base

"You do not need to leave your room. Remain sitting at your table and listen. Do not even listen, simply wait. Do not even wait, be quite still and solitary. The world will freely offer itself to you to be unmasked, it has no choice, it will roll in ecstasy at your feet."

Franz Kafka,
(Reprinted by permission of Schocken Books, Inc. from *The Great Wall of China* by Franz Kafka,©1946 by Schocken Books, Inc. Copyright renewed   1947 by Schocken Books, Inc.)

A. With Breathing as the Base

Remember to pick only *one* of the following ideas for each period of meditation.

1. Paying attention to Breathing
   a. Use your natural breathing as the base. Just watch it. Be aware of it. Don't influence it. Just as if you were watching a butterfly on a flower, its wings slowly going up and down, watch your breathing going up and down, in and out. If you need to, say silently to yourself, "In, out, in, out. . ."
   b. Or watch *or* feel your stomach or chest rising and falling with each breath. If you need to, silently repeat, "Rising, falling, rising, falling. . ."
   c. Or listen to the sound that your breath makes coming in and going out. If you want, include listening to the silence in between each breath.
   d. Or pay attention to the feeling or touch of the breath in your nose or throat or on your upper lip.

2. Counting the Breaths
   a. Count each inhalation or exhalation silently. Choose *one* of these counting methods:
      1. Count three breaths and then start over again.
      2. Count ten breaths and then start over again.
      3. Start at 200 and count backward, one for each breath.
   b. Or count as above, but also pay attention to listening to the sound of the numbers in your mind. Extend the number through each outbreath. Inhale, and as you breathe out, listen to your mind saying, "Onnnnnnne. . ." Inhale. "Twooooooo. . ." Inhale. "Threeeeeee. . ." Repeat.
   c. Or do the same, but visualize the numbers in your mind instead of listening to them.

3. Regulating the Breathing
   a. Make each breath the natural Yogic way, filling first the stomach, then the chest; emptying the chest first, then the stomach. Like filling and emptying a

glass of water. Pay attention to doing this.

b. Or time your breathing to your heartbeat as described on p. 77.

c. Or make each breath totally complete. Breathe in to your full capacity, and out till every last bit is expelled. Do this very slowly so you don't get hyperventilated, and read the section on breathing (p. 75) before you try this.

B. With Sound as the Base

1. Making Sounds

a. *Making sound aloud.* With each outbreath, hum. Make it a monotone so you don't get involved with composing melodies. Make it high *or* low, loud *or* soft, whatever feels right. Lips open or closed as you see fit, but be consistent. Pay attention to *letting* yourself make the sound and to listening to it.

b. *Making sound silently.* Same as above, but do it silently in your mind. You can time it with each breath or do it continuously. Just "mmmmmmmmmmmmmm. . ."

c. *Chanting.* Use one of the mantras described below and intone it monotonously over and over again throughout the meditation period. Again, *let* yourself make the sound. Don't try to do it. Just listen to yourself doing it. If a monotone is just too oppressive, make it a *very* simple melody. No more than three notes, and the same each time. You can also chant as a "stretch" before silent meditation. Chant aloud for five minutes or so, then stop and listen to the silence.

2. Listening to Sounds

a. *Specific sounds.*

1. Do one of the sound-making activities above, but specifically focus your attention on *listening* to it. Hear it clearly, without any judgment.

2. External sounds. Choose a specific sound outside yourself to hear clearly. It could be flies buzzing, water dripping, rain falling, traffic passing, ocean waves, a metronome, someone else's breathing or movements, footsteps, children playing, or whatever. The other evening I sat on our porch and used the crickets as a base. Beautiful.

3. Music. Music is tricky. It is good to use as a base if it doesn't absorb you so much that it traps your awareness. It's very seductive, and it may take you off into fantasy. You can keep it sort of uninvolving by only using very simple melodies, or you can work out a combination. Like letting your breathing go in time to the music, or watching your body move to it. If you keep getting lost in it, switch to another method.

b. *Sounds in general.* Just pay attention to whatever sounds occur. All the sounds in your environment. Don't try to label them. Just listen to them all.

With some practice, you may get a sense of the
basic silence behind all sounds. The silence which
forms the background or field upon which sounds
occur. You can listen to *that* as a focus if you wish.
Or you can listen to the tiny spaces of silence
between sounds. The use of sounds as a base is a
good thing to do in noisy settings. Then the sounds
which normally would be "distractions" become
the focus for meditation.

3. Mantra

A mantra (pronounced "mahntrah") is a specific sound,
word or phrase used for meditation. Mantras come in all
shapes and sizes. In some traditions they're given magical
powers. In others, they're a form of prayer. They can be
chanted aloud or recited silently. They are always repetitive.
In some Buddhist traditions they're written on paper and
spun round on a prayer wheel, with each revolution being
like a recitation. There are some modern mantras which
occasionally go unrecognized. The rosary, the Hail Marys
and the Our Fathers of Catholicism are mantras. "Alleluia"
and "Holy" and "Amen" are sometimes mantras when sung
repeatedly. You may be able to find some others if you look
around. Sometimes the meaning of the mantra word or
phrase becomes important, but we will concentrate on the
importance of the *sound* here.

Different sounds have different effects on awareness.
Some low sonorous monotones make you feel drowsy. Some
light, clear sounds tend to wake you up. Some screechy or
choppy sounds make you feel tense, while more flowing,
gentle sounds help you relax. Just for fun, relax a bit and
repeat this sound silently to yourself with your eyes closed,
and see how it makes you feel:

RRRRRRRRRRRRRRRRRRRR

Try this one:

ACK—ACK—ACK—ACK—ACK—ACK—ACK

And this one:

RAHLIM, RAHLIM, RAHLIM, RAHLIM

And this one:

HUMBER, HUMBER, HUMBER, HUMBER

I'm not suggesting any of these as mantras, but you can
sense the difference in how they make you feel. When you
choose a mantra as a base, pay attention to its effect on your
feelings and consciousness. You want one which encourages
bright awareness and relaxation at the same time.

The "TM" people make a big deal about your getting
the "right" mantra for yourself—and they subtly indicate
you'll be in a peck of trouble if you get the "wrong" one. It
is important, but I'm not sure that it's so critical that one has
to make everything top secret as they do. Besides, I assume
that you yourself can tell whether something is helping your
relaxation and awareness or not if you just use your common
sense. "TM" has struggled long and hard to keep its mantras
secret, and when the *Washington Post* published a whole
mess of them in September 1975, it must have seemed like
Pentagon Papers time at the Maharishi's TM centers all over

the world. Another cat out of the bag. It's also hard for me
to believe that there is just one "right" mantra for you.
Sufism, Buddhism and Hinduism all have stories that speak
to that point. Christianity too. One of them tells of a poor
hermit, way out in the boondocks, who took it upon himself
to recite one specific mantra for his entire life. Let's say it
was "GATÉ, GATÉ PARAGATÉ, PARASAMGATÉ,
BODHI SVAHA" which means "Gone, Gone, Gone Beyond,
Gone Totally Beyond, Salute." It comes from the Heart Sutra,
one of the most beautiful Buddhist scriptures. So this old guy
was chanting it, day in and day out, year after year. It
calmed him and cleared him so much that he was able to call
the thunder out of the sky, walk on water and do all sorts of
other neat things, or so the story goes. Then one day he was
visited by some monks from a faraway temple. They heard
him chanting the mantra and one turned to the other and
said, "Hey, this guy's got it all wrong. He's not pronouncing
the words right at all." So they decided to help him out and
teach him the right way. The hermit, very happy to have
been instructed in the correct pronunciation, thanked them
profusely. After that, he said it correctly. And the next time
he went to walk on the water, he sank.

I've known some people who got their "TM" mantra
and just couldn't stand it. Either the sound made them feel
bad or some association to it kept getting in the way. One of
my co-workers in a drug abuse program got a mantra which
sounded so much like "heroin" that he could hardly deal
with it. He kept thinking of work or getting high on drugs.
He had a good sense of humor, and spent most of his
meditation chuckling to himself. Which wasn't so bad after
all. Use your common sense.

There's a big difference between mantras that are
recited aloud or used as chants, and those which are repeated
silently in the mind. Those that are used aloud can take a lot
of abuse. You can fool around with them, and change them
from time to time as you wish. The silent ones take more
care, and should be handled with some attitude of reverence
and respect. Because with time they go deeply, deeply into
you. Spend enough time with a silent mantra and it becomes
an ongoing, never-ending part of you, as intimate as your
very heart. An example of this is the Jesus Prayer, one of the
purest Christian mantras. It is known as the Prayer of the
Heart because it is allowed to penetrate so silently and deeply
that it becomes one with the individual's very being. You
don't have to let your silent mantra go that deep, but if you
are going to, I think you should spend at least a year or two
in learning about your awareness through meditation before
you choose it.

In the meantime, you can try several and see whether
they act as helpful bases for you. It is O.K. to say them
aloud, too, as long as you're not letting them become heart-
prayers. The thing to remember about silent mantra is that
you just sort of "plant" it in your mind and then let it go.
Let it repeat by itself. You just watch it and listen to it. Let it
do what it wants. It may change in pitch, rhythm, or even in

its basic sound. Let it be. Just watch and listen.

The following are suggestions for mantras you can use, either aloud in chanting or silently by planting them. Some of them have meaning, some don't. If they do, and you can comfortably let it be, feel free to use them. If the meaning gets you carried away somewhere or turns you off in some way, try another one. If you chant them aloud, give yourself full rein to make the sounds full, deep, resonant and sonorous. Remember to keep it as much of a monotone as is comfortable. Low and full and easy, not squeaky or screechy and tight.

a. *Pure "root" sounds*
OM, pronounced "Ohm," or "Ahhowmm"
HUM, pronounced "Hooooooom"
AH, pronounced "Ahhhhhhhh"
HU, pronounced "Huuuuuuuu"

b. *Word-sounds that mean something like "peace"*
PEACE
SHALOM, pronounced "Shahlohmmm"
SHALEM, pronounced "Shahlaimmm"
SALAAM, pronounced "Slahmmm"
SHANTIH, pronounced with "a" as in "ah"
and "i" as in "wit"

c. *English words and phrases*

d. *The names of God*
In English, Hebrew, Sanskrit, Greek,
Arabic, or any other language.

e. *Tried and true Eastern mantras*

Om Mani Padme Hum Hri ཨོཾ་མ་ཎི་པདྨེ་ཧྲཱི

This is a very basic mantra which is related to compassion and refers to "the Jewel in the Lotus." It can be a salute to awareness, clear and free, out of which true compassion springs. Compassion is love with all desire, control, will, self/other and body/mind subtracted from it. It springs spontaneously from the very reality of any situation. But I don't want this to be a sermon. And the sound is most important. The pronunciation of the mantra varies. Padme can be either "pahdmay" or "paidmah." Mani is "mahney," and Hri is "ree." Om and Hum are pronounced above. I give you these pronunciations just in case you're as insanely perfectionistic as I am. But it really doesn't matter, because you're going to let the sound do what it wants anyway, right?

Κύριε Ιησού Χριστέ υιέ Θεού. Ἐλέησόν, μέ τόν, ἀμαρτωλόν.

Kirié Iiesou Christé yie Theoo Eleison me ton Amartalon.

This is the Jesus Prayer, in its entirety, in Greek. It has been mentioned above. The full English translation is "Lord Jesus Christ, Son of God, have mercy on me, a sinner." That's just too much Jesus and sin and stuff for a lot of people. As I said before, if your associations are going to carry you away from the sound, use another mantra. Or some other base entirely. But listen to the beautiful sound of the Greek words before you move on. "Keeriah eeusoo Kristay, eah thay-oo, eahlaysone may tone, ahmartalone."

Usually, the prayer is shortened to "Lord Jesus Christ, have mercy on me." Or just "Lord, have mercy." The old Eastern desert fathers set it silently to breathing. "Lord Jesus Christ" on the inbreath, "have mercy on me" on the outbreath.

Om   **Ah**   **Hum**

A combination of root syllables which is helpful in its simplicity. Very nice out loud. You can take one breath for each syllable, which is just like counting your breaths by threes, or you can put them all into one breath with no trouble. The pronunciations have been given above.

La Illaha Illa 'lla' Hu

From Islam, "There is no God but God." Out loud, melodic wafting sounds of vowels. Silently, in time and in touch with breathing or swaying of your head. Soft vowels throughout, with the "Hu" being "hoooo." All "A's" are "Ahh."

f. *Home-made mantras*

The nicest, sweetest mantra I ever used was one I conjured up in a very convoluted way a long time ago, before I knew much at all about mantras. I got very quiet, scribbled out an alphabet in random places on a sheet of paper with my eyes closed, then numbered 1-6 on the paper, again randomly with eyes closed. The six letters which came up, in sequence, were:

MIAHAE

I liked it. It sounded sort of liltingly Hawaiian, and it sailed silently through my mind in the most caressing way. Later on I got a TM mantra which seemed to relax me more, but never washed my awareness as clean and clear as did MIAHAE. The gimmick with the alphabet on the paper was just spur-of-the-moment fooling around, and I've never done it again. Once was letting be. Again would be trying.

There are all sorts of ways you can come up with your own mantra. One possibility is to get very relaxed and quiet, and then tell yourself that you're going to count down backward from ten to zero. Suggest to yourself that when you reach zero a silent word, sound or phrase will pop into your mind. Then you relax some more, take two or three deep breaths, and begin the countdown. Very slowly. When you hit zero, sure enough there it will be, big as life. I've done this several times. Occasionally they've been words with meaning, but most often they've been nonsense syllables. And they have always "worked" well for me in meditation; or you can pray for a word to come to you.

You can play with this business. Take it lightly. If it starts to feel very special and mystical, or if it seems to have great potential, forget it. Don't let anything get in the way of your objective —freeing awareness. You can tell whether what you're doing is trapping awareness or not—just stop for a moment and see how in touch you are with now.

With Visual Image as the Base

"While with an eye made quiet by the
      power
Of harmony, and the deep power of joy
We see into the life of things."
William Wordsworth, *Lines Composed
      a Few Miles Above Tintern Abbey*

Two ways
There are two ways of using a visual image as the base
for meditation. In the first, you actually look at some object.
In the second, you make up a mental image of something
and keep that in your awareness.

A. Looking at Something

Watching
Pick something to look at. In the chapter on
centering we used the example of a candle flame, which is a
very good object to start with. There is a specifically Hebrew
form of meditation in which one attempts to see certain
sacred letters in the flame. In other traditions, the flame
represents the sacred light which illuminates the dark
corners of our ignorance. But it is not necessary that the
flame symbolize anything. It could as well just be a candle
flame and nothing more.

Almost anything can be used as a visual base. If you are
coming from a Jewish tradition you might wish to use certain
Hebrew letters or words or a star of David. You can draw
them on a piece of paper and look at them. A Christian
might want to use a cross or a picture of Jesus or of some
saint who has special meaning. People who feel an affinity
for Islam or the Sufi tradition could use an image of a heart
or the name "Allah" written out in either English or Arabic.
There's also the Taoist Yin-Yang symbol. Hinduism and
Buddhism have all sorts of things to use as visual meditation
bases. Statues, pictures of gurus and deities, and those
wonderfully intricate mandalas and tankhas. Upon seeing a
Buddhist monk sitting before a statue of Buddha or a picture
of some saint, many westerners would assume that he was
"worshipping" the image. Probably not. Most likely, he is
using it as a base for free and formless meditation.

All of the objects I've mentioned so far have some
special meaning or symbolic significance to the people who
use them. As I indicated, this significance is not at all
necessary. As a matter of fact, it may get in the way of your
meditation if the importance of the image traps your
awareness. Here again, I think the simpler the object, the
better. Use anything you want, but I will give you a few
ideas.

Candle	Picture	The Sky	A Bug	Spot of Sunlight
Flower Tree	The Ocean	A Leaf	Picture	Smoke from Incense
Blank Wall	Clouds	Some Scene in Nature		Your Hand
A Pebble	A Star			

As you can see, there's no end to the possibilities. Get yourself positioned at a comfortable viewing distance from the object. Then just look at it. Don't scrutinize it, label it, judge it, or anything. Just look at it. Pay attention to it without shutting anything else out. Simply be interested in it. When you go off somewhere in your head, just come gently back to the object. Don't mess with your eyes. Don't try not to blink. Don't stare. Don't squint. If your eyes get tired, close them for a while and rest them. Just comfortably look. Let the object be. Keep your grubby hands off. It may well be that you have never looked at anything this way before. If so, it will be a revealing experience. As you are looking the object will seem to change. Let it change any way it wants. Don't get excited or afraid. Just passively watch.

There are two specific visual object-meditations which I want to discuss at some further length. They are not to begin with. You need some experience in letting-be before you do these. Practice some of the other ones first till you can let all the changes come and go without getting involved. The first is one in which you use your image in a mirror as an object.

Your image This is a good exercise, because you have a stronger tendency to manipulate or judge the reflection and so it's a good method of seeing how open you can be to it. If you really relax and spend more time than usual with this one, the image will change rather markedly. It may intrigue you, fascinate you, or frighten you. So as time goes on, it becomes more and more of a test of your letting-be ability. Whatever seems to appear in the mirror, just let it be. Neither hold it nor run away, just let it come and go. If you need some explanation of what happens, it will suffice to say that all you see in the mirror is a reflection of your various images of yourself. Many of these you will not have been previously aware of. That's O.K., too. *Please* don't make a big psychiatric analytical thing out of it. Don't worry about interpreting what you see. If you want to free awareness you have to let things be. If you interpret what you experience, that is *not* letting it be. And it compounds the difficulty, because then you must let the interpretation be. So it's much better just to watch and see. If you can.

Another person The second special visual-object experience is to use another person to look at. The two of you team up in the meditation by using each other as visual bases. You can pick one part of the other person to look at, like the eyes or face, or you can just let your eyes see the whole person. There may be a little anxious social stuff at the beginning like winks or giggles, but you just go right through that. Move toward just watching. Keep it silent, receptive. Again, the face will change, and there will be all sorts of emotionally exciting feelings. Don't get hooked or sidetracked by any of them. Just let them come and go. There will probably be feelings of attraction, repulsion, affection, dislike, sexual feelings, competitive feelings, scary feelings. Just let them all come and go. Keep your awareness free. Nothing else matters.

B. Watching a Mental Image

Imagining You do this either with your eyes closed or with them comfortably open facing a blank wall. The first way is to combine this with the previous technique of looking at something. Let's say you're using a flower as a base. You've been looking at it for some time, and things have become very quiet. Close your eyes, and conjure up a mental image of the flower, and use that as your base. Some people have no trouble at all in creating pictures in their minds. For others, it's not so easy. There's nothing special about being able to do it, so don't worry if you find it difficult. The idea is that you don't try to make it as though the object is really there, projected on the back of your eyelids. Just *imagine* it. Pretend it.

See how you are at this right now. Look at this design for a few minutes:

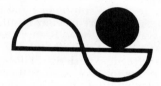

Now close your eyes and try to imagine it in your mind. Just pretend it's there. Can you sense it there? If not, try this: keep your eyes closed and silently describe it to yourself. Say, "The upper left-hand corner is shaped like. . . ." Just describe a little bit at a time. Talk out loud, if it helps, as though you were describing it to another person. See if this helps it get more clear. Even if you were able to picture it in your mind, it might help to go through this description process to get the image clearer. Still no good? Then try another tack. Think of your bathroom. See if you can picture it in your mind. Where is everything in there? What are the colors of everything? Get a sense of it in your mind. You can do that all right. You see, it's not a real *picture* in your mind. Just a sense of it is enough. It's like a memory. Remember the face of someone you knew in school and haven't seen for a while. Remember the house where you lived as a child. Remember sitting at the dinner table last night. Get the idea? That's the kind of mental image or sense that you nurture. If you've been looking at a flower for a while, all you need to do is close your eyes and *remember* it. It needn't take a lot of effort. Now it's true that if you do this a lot, nurturing this kind of memory-image or fostering any kind of image in your mind, the pictures will get clearer and clearer. But that's not important. It doesn't matter. If you do it a whole lot, or for an extended period of time, sooner or later you'll be surprised to find that the image *is* there, painted in three-dimensional living color on the back of your eyelids. Some traditions make a big deal of this, but it's nothing to brag about. Who goes around saying, "Hey, you know what I can do? I can see my

bathroom just as clear as day on the back of my eyelids!" It
doesn't matter. All you need for a mental image meditation
base is a sense or a memory of the object. As a matter of fact,
the chances of its kidnapping your awareness are less if it's
not too clear anyway.

Combination
So you can switch from actually looking at an object for
your base to watching your mental image or memory of it.
Or you can start out with a fresh mental image to use as a
base. Again, the sky's the limit on what you might choose
for this. You might want to use a little more care, though, in
picking something for a mental image than in just looking at
something. It's like the silent mantra compared to the out-
loud one. The one in your mind is more intimate. It can
become a part of you. So maybe don't use your bathroom as
a mental image base. But there still are innumerable other
things. You could make mental images of all the real objects
I mentioned before. And what's especially nice is that if you
love the seashore, for example, but you're not near the
seashore, you can be there in your mind. Or in outer space if
you like. But watch out, now. Remember your objective.
This is just for a base. You're not going *away* on a trip to
have a nice daydream experience. You just want a simple
base to come *home* to. As I've said, there's a whole set of
trance-and-travel meditation approaches where you can
entertain yourself this way if you want. In the open way
however, it's nothing but a base to help us free our
awareness right here and right now.

Sound
Visual images are also good to combine with other
bases, such as sound. The Om Mani Padme Hum Hri chant
goes with the visualization of a lotus, upside down on top of
your head, the fluid nectar of compassion dripping from the
flower down into you, filling you completely, then
overflowing from you, filling your immediate environment,
and then on and out to the rest of your land, the planet
earth, till the whole cosmos is filled with compassion, all
occurring in the form of a mental image as you're chanting
away. If you want, you can use a circle of light, like a crown
above your head illuminating you, then your surroundings
with the light of compassion. Both of these are worth
spending some time with. It may be a bit difficult the first
time. Or it may seem a little absurd. But don't judge too
swiftly. The first time I tried this I was in a group and I
remember looking across at some of my friends during the
chant. These usually dignified ladies and gentlemen, I
imagined, were sitting there with silly-looking flowers stuck
upside down at odd angles on their heads. I was chanting
"Om, Mani (giggle) Padme (Ha Ha) Hum Hri (Hee Hee
Hee)." But after a while I got settled down and there was
something incredibly quiet and strong and open going on.
With practice, it became even more meaningful, though I
still giggle at the flowers sometimes.

Unusual developments
Another friend of mine was doing well with the chant
until he started filling up with nectar. He sprang a leak
somewhere in his legs and all the nectar kept running out of
him. You see, the visualizations sometimes take a course of

their own. Another one that happened to me was in an exercise where I was chanting "Ahhhhhh" and visualizing a crystal ball of light suspended inside my head between my eyebrows. Part of this exercise is to roll your head around while you chant and visualize the ball of light. At one point, my ball of light broke loose and started careening around the inside of my skull like a roulette ball. Again it broke me up laughing. These crazy developments in visualizations are, I think, simply more inventive ways that the mind uses to keep you from quietness. But if they're going to happen, there's nothing wrong with chuckling about them a little.

Out of the head   Once you have become comfortable with keeping a visual image in your mind, you might want to move it out of your head a bit. The head is where we generally think of being, the domicile of our "self." So most of us, seeing a visual image, feel as if we are seeing it in our heads. This is really a quite restrictive and discriminatory attitude, for if we exist at all, we exist far beyond our skulls. So try visualizing an image and see it in your stomach. Or in your heart. It will be a little difficult at first, but it will help loosen your frozen ideas about where you reside.

Chapter Twenty

Words: Scripture, Koan and Prayer

"Let the words of my mouth, and the meditation of my heart, be acceptable in thy sight, O Lord, my strength and my redeemer."
Psalm 19:14

A. With Scripture or Koan as Base

Written words   Religious scripture, verses, passages of poetry or other literature can be good bases. The excerpt should be quite short—again, the simpler the better. There are several ways to go about this.

   a. Copy your selection on a piece of paper and use it as a visual base by watching it, reading it gently again and again.
   b. Read it aloud repeatedly and listen.
   c. Read it aloud several times to plant it in your mind, then watch it going on there. If you wish, you can keep it going all the time and use it for informal meditation, too.
   d. Read it just once or twice, then sit back and let your mind go where it wants to with it.
   e. If it describes a scene, a person, an event, or an object, visualize that in your mind and use that as a base. Let the story continue in your mind.
   f. Memorize a short piece of poetry, plant it in your mind, and listen.

There are other ways with which you can experiment. You will note, however, that this form of using a written piece as a base does not involve much intentional thinking *about* it, analyzing it, or trying to figure out what it means. You just allow it to take you wherever it decides to take you.

Koans   On the other hand you *can* try to figure out a Koan. The word "Koan" comes from a Zen Buddhist tradition. In this tradition, the Koan is seen as one of the most effective tools for freeing awareness. Generally, a Koan is a statement, a question, or a problem which one tries to understand. But they don't have intellectual answers. You've probably heard the Koan "What is the sound of one hand clapping?" The Zen assignment is to plant the statement or question inside yourself, not just in your mind but down deep in your belly as well, and hang in there with it till you get the answer. In many Zen traditions, the work with Koan is very effortful—involving much struggle and concentration. I don't recommend you try this unless you have very good guidance. Effortful meditation can mess up your mind in quite unpleasant ways. But it is possible to work with a Koan effortlessly, and some people have found this very helpful. One way is to plant a question, or a brief piece of scripture or literature in your mind, as suggested in "c" above. Then, when it's going along in your mind pretty much by itself, begin to ask what it means. What is the answer? You can just ask those questions and then wait. Wait till the sense of

an answer comes to you. Don't try to put it in words or
concepts. Just a sense of its meaning. Then pay attention to
that and see if it deepens, changes, or disappears. Remember
again though that getting the answer is not your goal in open
meditation. You use the Koan as a base, when you need it.

The other way to use a Koan is even more tricky, as you
are even more likely to start working at it and losing your
awareness in it. But some people can do this well and find it
helpful. You plant the question as before, and then *allow*
your mind, your intellect, to try to figure out the answer.
You let yourself explore it conceptually and try to make
sense of it. But you need to watch your mind doing this.
Watching your mind trying to figure it out is the base. It's
very subtle, and if you can't keep that impartial observation
of your mind going, if your awareness keeps getting trapped
in the attempt to find an answer, you'd better use another
method. I can't handle this one myself—and I'm not really
interested in this method anyway. But I include it because
some people find it helpful.

Some Koans which you might want to consider:
From the Judaeo-Christian Lineage:

> I Am That I Am. Ehyeh Asher Ehyeh. (Exodus)

> In order to arrive at knowing everything, desire
> to know nothing. (St. John of the Cross)

> The least among you all, he is the greatest. (Luke)

> In every place where you find the imprint of
> men's feet, there am I. (Talmud)

> Be assured of this, that you must live a dying
life. (Thomas à Kempis)

> What is self-contradiction? (Martin Buber)

From Eastern Traditions:

> It is not mind which we should want to know. We
> should know the Thinker. (Kaushitaki Upanishad)

> How can the knower be known? (Brihad-
> aranyaka Upanishad)

> Gain or Loss: which is more painful? (Tao
> Te Ching)

> Without speaking, without silence, how can
> you express the truth? (Zen)

> What was the nature of your being before
> your parents were born? (Zen)

> All this is not mine, I am not this,
> this is not myself. (Buddhism)

Most people see the function of a Koan as taking you beyond
your intellect; teaching you how to think, feel, sense with
your whole being rather than with just the rational part of
your mind. But a Koan can help you even further than this.

Used as a base for open meditation, it can take you to a level
of simplicity in which there is very little left to capture
awareness.

B. With Prayer as the Base

Some ways   Again, there are several ways. All of the forms
suggested for scripture can be used with prayer. Or:
  a. Use the Jesus Prayer as described under mantras.
  b. Use another formal prayer in the same way.
  c. Pray as you usually do, if you usually do, and then
     afterward just be still and listen. Listening openly
     is the base.
  d. Wait to hear what sort of spontaneous prayer will
     come up in you. Watching for this is the base. The
     prayer should be truly spontaneous—it should just
     sprout up. Which means you may sit there and
     nothing will happen. But don't get impatient and
     pushy. Wait and watch. Some people using this
     approach see it not as their praying but as God
     praying through them.

Personal   This one was very meaningful to me. I prayed a lot as a
experiences little kid, but after I got out of college I stopped. I was angry
at the church, and God didn't seem to be around anymore,
sort of like the tooth fairy, and besides I had medicine to
study. Prayer was childish, I thought, and I'd be damned if
anyone would catch me at it. Except, of course, for those
secret little times we don't talk about. Like when I'd get
really scared or worried or someone close to me was dying,
or when I really wanted something *awfully* bad. Then
there'd be that sneaky little-boy voice inside the
sophisticated doctor that would be pleading, "Dear God,
please." It would sort of slip out. I couldn't help it. Like a
burp in church. When I'd catch myself at that, it would sort
of disgust me. "How very childish," I'd say, and strengthen
my resolve to be more mature.

   That kind of thing went on for years. There were
occasions when I'd feel nostalgic or philosophical or
something, and seriously try to pray. But it would never
work. I felt I had to believe in God in order to pray, and I
really didn't. I felt I had to have some idea about God in
order to pray, and I didn't. All there was was stuff like "The
process of the Universe," "The cosmic sequence of events,"
or "The ground of being." None of which I could get my
head around enough to pray to it. So I gave up.

   A couple years after I started meditating, I very
gradually started to pray again. Unintentionally, with no fear
or pain or sruggle. When in meditation there was no desire
to pray and no desire not to pray, prayer simply started
to happen. I still had no trustworthy concept of God, but
that didn't matter somehow. The prayer was happening.
I didn't do it, I let it. Now, I'm very comfortable with prayer,
and I both do it and let it, and I still haven't any concept of
God. I'm not even trying to get one, because I'm sure it would
be wrong anyway.

Chapter Twenty-One

With the Body as Base

"If anything is sacred the human body is sacred."
Walt Whitman,
Leaves of Grass

Whole body movement

Some people are simply body-people. They relate to the world with their bodies. For them, no number of words or concepts can match a simple dance. Just saying "I love you" is not enough for them. They've got to be hugged. For them, a body base for meditation may be just right.

Classically patterned movements such as those of Tai Chi or Yoga are excellent. So are freely flowing spontaneous movements. One way is to begin in a standing position. Stand up straight and relax. "Tune in" to the position and sensations of your body. Breathe deeply and slowly, and feel it. Then slowly begin to move, however it feels comfortable and right. You can move your whole body, as in a spontaneous dance, or you can just move your hands or head or trunk. Experiment both with free, ever-changing movements and with repetitive movements. All the while, pay attention to everything your body is feeling. Sense it all. Keep sharp and clear in your awareness. Keep it slow.

If you want, do the movements to music. But its best to work toward doing them in silence. A good thing to set up might be a short period of music on record or tape that you can switch off after five or ten minutes, so you can start off to music and then flow into silence.

After you've moved for what seems long enough, get comfortably seated and continue to pay attention to how your body feels. Use the body sensations as a base. If you lose "touch" with your body sensations during the time you're sitting, you can tune in again by making slow easy movements with your hands or head, or letting your trunk sway back and forth a little. But only if you need to. Ideally, you will just sense the feeling of stillness in your body after the movement, like you sense the silence after a chant.

The Dance of your hands

Another approach is to watch the movements of your hands. Sit comfortably and look at your hands. Let them begin to move, slowly, spontaneously. Notice the way one moves in relationship to the other. Sense how they feel. Look at the space between them. It will begin to seem as if it has substance. See also how they move through space. Let them go and just watch. You can do this for the entire meditation period, just paying attention to them when you need to. They are the base. Or you can just move them for a few minutes and then let them rest, but you still use their feelings as the base.

Walking

Walking can be a good base too. I remember going on a "meditation walk" with my kids last winter when it snowed. We agreed to be silent, and to pay attention to our feet moving and to just let all the sensations of snow and countryside and cold come into our awareness without holding on to any of them. It was an incredibly lovely experience. I find myself doing it spontaneously now sometimes. It has become part of my informal meditation.

Body watching massage

Another possibility is to pay attention to the stillness or spontaneous movements of one specific part of the body. Choose one and stick with it. For example, pay attention to how your eyes move or don't move during meditation. Or your eyelids. Or your tongue. Or one finger.

Massage can also be a good form of meditation. Very slowly massage the muscles in your face, neck, shoulders, arms, hands and feet. Pay attention to the sensations. Then rest and be aware of what your body is feeling.

Hara

Still another option is to spend some time with *Hara* or *Kuf,* the center point of the body. This is the body's center of gravity, located about two inches below your navel. It is of great significance in many spiritual traditions, and is worthy of your attention for a while. It is sometimes difficult for us head-oriented westerners to pay attention to our bellies other than by feeding them. But there are several ways of going about it, and the experience is fresh.

First, move around the room spontaneously and sense what part of the body seems to be leading the movements. From what part do the movements seem to be originating? For many people it's up high, around the head or shoulders. Once you've identified the leading spot, let it slip down to your center point, and then allow all your movements to come from there.

If this is difficult to conceptualize, try another way. Stand upright with your feet slightly apart and knees slightly bent. Your weight should be distributed equally on both feet. Think about that spot just beneath your belly button. Then slowly let your weight shift from your left foot to your right. As if it were heavy sand, running up your leg from your left foot, *through* the center point and down your right leg into your left foot. Be aware of the center point while this is happening. Then when all the weight is in your right foot, lift the left foot up lightly and freely and set it down in front of you. *After* your left foot is on the ground, let the weight flow back through the center point and into that left foot. Move around this way a little. Don't worry if it looks funny at the beginning. What you're doing is centering your body's attention right where it ought to be—at the center of gravity.

Another image which some people have found helpful is to picture an almost-full glass of water sitting right inside the lower abdomen. As you move, don't let the water spill.

When you have a sense of the center point, sit down and pay attention to it. Not quite contemplating your navel, but about two inches below it. Let that stomach area fill out each time you breathe in. Let your breath go right down to that point and back out again. That's where your body's centered and that's where your attention can be centered as well.

However you "use" your body as a base for formal
meditation, you will find it especially helpful in informal
meditation as well. Your body is always with you, always
there for you to sense, to merge with in completeness in any
activity.

Chapter Twenty-Two

With Miscellaneous Senses as the Base

"How good is man's life, the mere living!
　　how fit to employ
All the heart and the soul and the
　　senses forever in joy!"

Robert Browning,
Saul

We've really been talking about using senses as a base all along. Sound is really using the auditory sense. The visual image-base is sight. The body bases use touch and position sense as well as vision. Later on we'll talk about using your "sixth" or mental sense as the base.

But there are a few miscellaneous sense-bases that **Other** should be mentioned, because it's just possible that one of **senses** them might be very helpful to you.

a. *Smell.* If you burn incense or are fortunate enough to have some flower or blossom-fragrance around, you can use that as a base. An orange grove in bloom is incredible. So are lilacs. Or fresh hay. Or a wood fire. If you can hone up your awareness sharply, you don't even need a special aroma to pay attention to. You can just sense whatever aromas come by. Remember, whether you like it or not doesn't matter, right? So if you're sitting on a hillside sniffing the breeze and some dodo happens to be walking his dog upwind of you, that's just fine, right? You let it be. No labels. No judgment. Just sniff.

b. *Touch.* Many touch-objects can be good bases. The touch of a breeze on your hair and skin, the touch of water on your feet, the touch of the cushion on your sitting bones. Or you can softly stroke a piece of wood or stone. We have some guinea pigs which are very nice because they have the softest fur and they sit absolutely still when you pet them. That's another kind of touch base. Use your imagination.

c. *Taste.* There's no reason you couldn't use taste as a base as well. Suck on a candy or sip a soft drink. When it's gone, use your search for the lingering taste as a base.

d. *With "distractions" as base.* All things which seem to be distracting come through your senses. Whether the distraction is a thought or an itch or a sound, it comes into awareness through the channels of your senses. If during meditation you find that one special "distraction" is repeatedly kidnapping your attention, it is often helpful to go ahead and use that distraction as the base for your meditation. Go ahead and pay attention to it. Then it can't be a "distraction" anymore.

Recently a young man told me he was having trouble meditating because of a toothache. So he used the pain as a base for attention and everything went beautifully. The pain didn't go away entirely, but he stopped suffering with it.

The same goes for loud sounds, persistent thoughts, troublesome emotions, whatever. There is a beautiful flexibility in this, and it comes very close to the basic practice of allowing mind to be what it is.

In the process of using distraction as base it may well happen that the distraction will disappear entirely. Sometimes my knees hurt while I'm sitting, so I'll pay attention to that and after a while the pain is gone. Or sometimes if I'm angry about something I'll use the anger as a base, and it will up and disappear. This is just something which happens sometimes. When you pay relaxed attention to something, you tend to become one with it, and then there's nobody left for it to irritate. So it just quits.

Powerless power

Discovering this, it is tempting to try to pay attention to a discomfort *in order to get rid of it*. But that doesn't work. There's too much willful manipulation involved. So it's best not even to try. But try you probably will, for there is a sense of power in it. "Ah, I'll control my pain by accepting it," which is just the same as deciding "I'll get what I want by saying, 'Thy will be done.'" It is, I suppose, a cleansing sort of learning to experience the failure of this. And to discover that true power comes only to those who are truly powerless.

Chapter Twenty-Three

With Mind as Base

"Meditation is to be aware of thought, of feeling, never to
correct it, never to say it is right or wrong, never to justify it,
but just to watch it and move with it."
Krishnamurti, *Talks and Dialogues* (Avon, N.Y., 1970)
Quoted by permission of J. Krishnamurti, Krishnamurti Foundation
Trust Limited, London

All the bases so far have been using the usual five
senses as vehicles. These are the channels for what you see,
smell, touch (or feel), taste and hear. There is now another
sense which must be included. I will call it the "sixth" sense,
but it doesn't mean anything supernatural or paranormal.
It's simply the sense you have of what's going on in your
mind. Just as you see a flower or smell a fragrance or hear
the call of birds, you can sense the activities of your mind.
The thoughts, feelings, images, fantasies and memories
which rise and fall in your consciousness all the time. If I
asked you what you were thinking just now, you'd be able
to tell me. How do you know? Because you have some
awareness of what's been going on in your mind. Or if I ask
you to tell me what you feel like today, whether you're
happy or sad or whatever, you can sort of scan your mind,
review what's there and what's just been there, and you'd be
able to come up with a pretty accurate answer. So the sixth
sense is nothing special. You use it every time you say "I
think that . . ." or "It seems to me that . . ." or "I
remember . . ." or "I wish . . ." It's a very common and
natural thing. We all have it. It's just that we don't pay
attention to it very often.

Using mind as a base for meditation means moving into
this sixth sense in a keen and clear way. As with all the other
senses, relaxation is important if the channel is to be open.
We don't have to reach out or grab what we're aware of.
Simply relax and open up to what is there.

I've arranged the mind-bases into six categories. None
are terribly easy for "beginners," but I would suggest you
try a few. If nothing else, they will help you experience the
dynamic process of mind in ways which are probably fresh
for you.

I. The Mind Research Laboratory

In this category of bases you fully use your sixth sense
Light to examine mental events. Observe them closely. To do this,
research you have to adopt the attitude of a skilled and incisive
scientific researcher. Have no bias. Carry no hidden wish as
to how your research will come out. Don't fudge any of the
results. You simply observe and note what occurs. It doesn't
matter whether you "like" the results or not. You are just
cleanly and acutely scrutinizing mind. The danger of this
approach is that it's liable to reinforce one's crazy

assumption that there's me and there's my mind. It's too separating and objectifying. In order to minimize this, take it all very lightly and from time to time ask yourself who it is that is studying your mind. Some of the mind-research exercises can also be a bit scary, because they tend to bring one up very closely against one's self-image. Again, the only important thing is not to make anything too important. Don't push or pull on your mind in any way. Just gently watch.

In any kind of research, there is always the problem that the scientist will interfere with the study simply because of his or her presence. What this means with mind is that as soon as you try to examine thoughts, your mind may decide not to produce any thoughts. Or when you look for feelings, there will be nothing but thoughts. The mind will change its behavior just because you're looking.

The twerts As an example of this scientific-research problem, let's say you've decided to study the mating habits of North American long-tailed twerts. You've captured two of the little creatures and have them sitting in front of you on the laboratory table. You watch them, and they look at each other, and then they look at you. Nothing happens. You're not learning anything, except perhaps that twerts don't like to mate in public.

Probably it was your taking them out of their natural environment which made them change their behavior. So you decide to take them back to the forest and let them be in their natural habitat. Then you dress up in a camouflage suit and sneak through the woods to spy on them. There they are, nibbling on the grass, unaware of your presence. So far so good. Then one of them starts snuggling up to the other, purring sweet nothings. It's finally going to happen. You crane your neck and pull out your camera. But then you step on a twig or the wind shifts and they know you're there. Everything comes to a screeching halt.

It's just like that with your mind. If you're going to be accurate, you have to be very quiet, very still and very very patient. You must avoid interfering with the natural process of things. If you really want to see how twerts go about doing whatever they do, you would have to go to their place in the forest, pull up a stump, and sit very still. For a long time. Repeatedly. After a while, the twerts will peek out and look at you. You don't do anything. Just sit there. Sooner or later, they'll get used to your presence. You'll be like another tree in the forest. And if you have enough patience and can sit waiting very still, they will come out and begin to behave quite naturally. But even when they start performing you can't show any interest. If you really want to see them naturally, you can't do *anything* except sit and watch. This is the best way to observe twerts, and it is the best way to observe mind. It is perhaps idealistic to expect that we will have the extreme patience and quietness necessary for truly pure observation, but we can be as still and alert and non-reacting as possible. That's all anyone could ask; just be the best kind of scientist you can.

The process With all the following approaches to mind-research, it is probably best to begin with some time of physical relaxation, then some slow transition from being aware of your surroundings to being aware of your mind. One way of doing this is to spend some time simply counting your pulse or your breaths. Then when you're bright and clear with that, start picturing the numbers in your mind as you count. Or listen to the sound of the numbers. Then, when that's going well, quit the counting and proceed with observing mind.

A. *Categorizing mental events.* Take note of the different kinds of things that happen in your mind. That's your base. There will be thoughts, feelings, memories, fantasies, impulses, urges, images, what else? You can even make a list, *after* meditation. But remember that the goal here is not to gain a great deal of knowledge *about* mind. It is rather to use mind as a simple base for attention while you permit mind to be what it is. Whatever knowledge you acquire is of no value besides that of entertainment. But the wisdom of greatest value comes as you permit yourself to be who you are.

B. *Refining the categories.* Pick one kind of mental event, such as thoughts, and see what different forms it includes. For example, there are:

1. Loud, clear wordy thoughts.
2. Quiet, subtle thoughts that don't have words.
3. Automatic, stereotyped or robot-like thoughts.
4. Discussion-type thoughts, where you carry on a
   conversation with yourself.
5. Labeling thoughts (e.g., "That sound is a car horn").
6. Judgmental thoughts (e.g., "I'm not doing this very
   well").
7. Hopeful thoughts.
8. Worry thoughts.
9. Just hints of thoughts—thoughts that start to form
   but get silenced before they're born.

And so forth. Again, you can make a list, *after*. Or do the
same thing with memories or visual images, or any other
mental event.

C. *Comparing the categories.* Use, as a base, your
paying attention to the differences between mental events.
How does a feeling differ from a thought? A memory from
a fantasy, etc.? Don't get too conceptual. Don't spend too
much time thinking *about* the difference. Just *see* what the
difference *is*.

D. *Discovering where mental events come from, how
they arise.* Be very alert and see just how thoughts,
sensations, fantasies and other mental events arise. Just *how*
do they come into consciousness? Where were they
before? What point do they arise from? What makes them
happen? Again, don't get conceptual. Just *see* how they
arise.

E. *Counting mental events.* Pick one category, such as
thoughts, and count them in the same way you count
breaths. Or keep a running total for your meditation time. If
keeping the numbers in your mind creates a problem, sit
with pencil and paper and make a little mark for each one.
That way you can keep your eyes closed if you wish. Here
you must remember a little difference from the scientist.
Remember that your objective is free awareness, not an
accurate total.

F. *Open-eyed writing as a base.* Sit with pencil and
paper, and briefly note each mental event. No more than one
or two words for each one.

II. Watching the Clouds Roll By

The stream This process was already mentioned in the section on
mini-meditations as watching mental events as if they were
clouds in the sky. It's one of the best ways to use the mind
as base, but it is so simple that it may seem very difficult.
You just watch all the stuff that goes through your mind. All
the thoughts, images, sounds, sensations, memories,
impulses and feelings make up the "stream of
consciousness." You sit and watch that stream go by, just as
if you were watching a real stream with its ripples, currents,
eddies and floating leaves and twigs. Just watch them all
pass. Make no attempt to hold them, push them, control

them, or interpret them in any way. "Distraction" occurs
when one of those mental events captures your attention and
carries it downstream. When you recognize this, just let it go
and get back to watching.

III. Watching the Space Between Thoughts

The between   Mental events are like sounds. They are not totally
continuous. If you look closely and are very alert, you will
catch sight of tiny spaces in between the events. If you're
good and quiet, you can watch these little spaces as your
base. Or you can get a sense of the background, the screen
on which all the mental events are projected, and use that as
a base. It's like the silence which is the background for
sounds. What is it in the mind? Nothingness?
Emptiness? Pure consciousness? Does it have a sense of
form? Color? Texture? Depth? You can work on that
concept when you're not meditating. But when you're
meditating just watch it. Avoid any tendency to stretch the
space between thoughts or to keep the background pure. Just
watch.

IV. Watching the Watcher

The seer   More convoluted yet. You begin with watching your
thoughts or the space between them or something else in
your mind. Use a little effort to get a clear sense of *watching*.
Then start looking at the part of you which is watching.
Watch the watcher. You need to be in a very quiet, very
uninvolved, very peaceful position to do this, which is good.
If you find yourself working at it, quit and use another
approach.
     As a matter of fact, all of these mind-bases very easily
slip into being a lot of work. As such, you can use them to
give your mind a stretch before some quieter, more receptive
meditation. But if you use one of them as *the* meditation,
keep it as loose and easy as you can. Remember to use the
least possible effort.

V. Tenkan With Your Thoughts

Aikido   In the chapter on "Mind and Me" I described an Aikido
movement called *Tenkan*, in which one turns to the side and
steps in behind an onrushing opponent. In this way the
opponent's own force carries him away, and you simply
follow along behind, encouraging the direction of his
movement.
     Though thoughts are never really your opponents, it
often seems as if they are. If for example you feel that your
thoughts are continually attacking you, attempting to trap
your awareness or pull you off and away from here and
now, it is possible to do *tenkan* with your thoughts. If there
must be any battle at all with your thoughts, *tenkan* is a very
efficient and gentle way of going about it.
     With a real live physical attacker, the movements of

your feet are most important. You are standing with your
left foot in front, right foot behind and at right angles:

Weight is evenly distributed, and you are relaxed, comfortable and loose. You *stay* relaxed as the attacker charges.

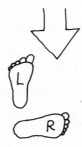

Just as the attacker gets to you, you turn to your right, simply by shifting your left foot and turning your pelvis. Then he passes right by in front of you. He comes very close, but he misses.

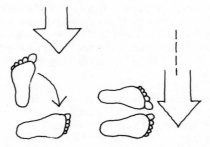

This may be all that's necessary. His force carries him off and away. But if he does catch hold of you, you just step in behind him and briefly go along with him as his momentum carries him past.

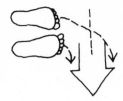

You needn't push on him or struggle in any way. Your simple shift of movement, your going with him, will help his momentum go forward and soon he'll tumble of his own accord. Then you simply resume your relaxed, comfortable stance.

Practice this with another person to get the physical feel of it, then sit down and do *tenkan* with your thoughts. Your attention is relaxed, comfortable. As a thought comes, just turn a little and let it pass on by. If it hooks you, move with it till it tumbles. All the way through you remain easy and loose. In physical Aikido there are other things you can do with *tenkan*, such as guiding the opponent's force in a circle till he trips himself up. But this is not necessary with thoughts. You need exert no force of your own. Just be so relaxed, alert and flexible that the force of your thoughts alone carries them off into unimportance.

VI. Moving Into Mind

No object All the preceding mind-bases are preparations for this one. This is where the distinction between you and your mind begins to blur. You are less and less concerned about watching. Begin by simply relaxing and turning attention to your mind. No interference. Whatever happens in mind, go with it, move into it, finally becoming one with it. No relationship. No objectification. Just dissolving yourself into what's happening. This takes a good deal of relaxing, and a lot of brightness. You cannot willfully become one with your mind, or with anything. Because if it's intentional you're still there doing it, and that inevitably keeps you separate. So the only possibility is to keep relaxing, opening more and more, and then, at some point, it will simply happen.

The Simplest of Bases

"O holy simplicity!"

The last words of Jan Huss,
at the stake, 1415

I. With the Here and Now as the Base

Here I am This is essentially the same process as that described in informal meditation. Only you're sitting still and not trying to *do* anything. Begin with the thought "Here I am." You can start off with using that phrase as a mantra. When something comes into consciousness, you can elaborate if you need to. "Here I am thinking about such-and-such." Everything that's happening is fair game. As soon as possible, drop the "Here," so it's just "I am . . . whatever." Then drop the description of what you're doing. Then it's just "I am." Then, when it happens, allow the "I" to go. At that point, you're just left with "am," which is the same as just "being." Finally, drop the thought of being and just be. All the words are just to make it possible for you to move more intimately into the experience. Let them all go as soon as you can. You don't want to make any of that stuff too important. Most especially, you don't want to make a big deal out of "I am."

II. With Awareness Itself as the Base

Aware of Simpler still. All you do is pay attention to being aware.
awareness Just sense awareness. Keep coming back to it. That's all.

III. With Everything and Nothing as the Base

All and none Either everything is the base or nothing is. It's the same either way. There's nothing to watch or pay attention to *especially*. Yet it's all there. You watch everything in general and nothing in particular. After a while, there is no idea of watching, no idea of doing anything, no idea of yourself. It is simply being aware. There is no real center. The center has expanded to include everything everywhere.

IV. Baseless Meditation

Real As the forms of meditation become simpler, there is less
meditation to say about them; they are virtually impossible to describe. Baseless meditation is the real thing. Real meditation. There may be the initial intent to sit down, but that's all the will or intentionality which occurs. There's no idea of meditating while the meditation happens. There is neither any doing nor any not-doing. This is even simpler than the basic practice, because you're not even in there giving permission for your mind to be. There are no distractions.

I could go on with a long list of what baseless meditation is *not*, but the only thing I can say about what it is, is that it is real meditation. If you imply from this that all the other forms are not real, you may be correct. But that doesn't mean they're not valuable. They are practice.

Practice pretending the simplicity of being. One could do worse.

Leftover stuff

The appendix is a vestigial organ. Not so much an afterthought as a leftover from times gone by. In the ancient evolutionary spiral of mankind, the human appendix once served some sort of useful function. Now it has none. Except perhaps to remind us of our past.

There is some similarity between the appendix of this book and the human one. This one is filled with vestigial material. Concepts and theories, word-pictures and stuff *about* being and awareness. All grossly inadequate, as are any words *about* anything. But since I still have vestigial, leftover parts of my mind which need to conceptualize about life, I assume others do too. And it is for this reason that the material herein is included. It has been helpful to me, as long as I didn't take it too seriously. Perhaps it will be to you as well.

The Entrapment of Human Awareness

A model

This is theory. A model of how awareness becomes trapped. A concept of it all. Models and concepts are at best inaccurate. They are like maps. A map tells you something about the terrain it describes, but it certainly is very unlike that terrain. When we're looking at a road map, we don't get the map confused with the terrain. We don't try to drive our car on the map. But when it comes to concepts about the mind or about awareness, we often do get confused. Freud made up a good concept model of the mind which included things like Ego, Id, and Superego. It wasn't long until his followers started thinking of these things as real. The concepts seemed to have taken on some substance and solidity. Sometimes when we're working with a client, we psychiatrists begin to sense that there actually *is* an ego in there which we can somehow influence. We forget that the ego, and even the mind itself, are concepts—just models of reality.

In a sense, that's no different than looking at the little red line on the road map, then getting into the car and trying to find a little red line to drive on. Theologians, most of them, understand how mistaken all of our concepts of God are. One of these days, the rest of us will understand how mistaken all of our concepts of the human mind are. Let's just remember that all the ideas which follow are just concepts and nothing more.

The personality

In order to make up a concept of what happens to awareness, we have to look at the development of the human personality as a whole. This means that we have to get very objective, and it means that I get very psychological. It also means that we must use metaphors extensively, because awareness is not something that is easily conceptualized.

There are five aspects of human personality which impinge upon awareness most importantly:
1. Desire
2. Control
3. The sense of self/other
4. The sense of body/mind
5. Will

Each of these is a concept in its own right. If we could just let them be without imposing any order on them, they would appear, sort of floating in our mind like sparkles in a vast field of awareness.

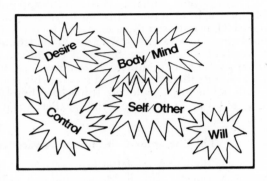

Flower image

But if we impose some order on them, we can get them arranged in a "meaningful" sequence. I have tried to be sort of cute and make awareness the center of a flower, with desire, control, etc., as the different petals which get stuck on it. I thought this might be appropriate inasmuch as it's somewhat similar to the oriental idea of a many-petaled lotus which gently unfurls till the pure awareness within comes free again. But mine came out looking more like an artichoke.

The image of a flower also communicates that the way awareness develops and becomes obscured is not so horrible. It's not what we have to call pathological. It's just what happens normally. The problems come when we overdo it, when we bind the petals together rigidly. The idea of the dotted line to the open flower indicates a gentle unfolding. A blooming which will take place if you let it. YOU CAN'T RIP THE PETALS APART. It's just a matter of not holding them so tightly.

The stages

Stage 1 of the diagram occurs sometime before birth and probably lasts until shortly after birth. The fetus has some awareness before birth. This awareness is at a pretty basic level. Certainly nothing special about it. The fetus probably doesn't even recognize any difference between sleeping and being awake.

Then, with the flooding of sensations and stimuli which occur at and shortly after birth, awareness becomes something special. This is Stage 2. Awareness isn't just awareness any more. It's AWARENESS! Now it seems that

1. Awareness

2. Awareness!

3. Desire

4. Control

5. Self/Other

6. Body/Mind

7. Will

the infant can sense a difference between waking and
sleeping. It even seems to enjoy its awareness.

Stage 3 also occurs within the first few days or weeks of
life. The infant experiences sensations which are clearly
comfort and discomfort, or pleasure and pain. Though its
responses to these sensations are still at a reflex level, this is
the beginning of *desire*. The baby wants something, like
milk, and it is uncomfortable till it gets it. The other side of
desire is wanting something to go away, like wetness in a
diaper or a scratch from a safety pin. Desire, in the form of
pain and pleasure, is the first petal which gets glued to the
infant's awareness. This is all very hypothetical, of course,
but if the infant could talk and you asked it what its
awareness was for, it might say something like, "To feel
good and not bad."

At the beginning, the infant's response to desire is
reflexive. If it is uncomfortable, it cries and wiggles. If it
feels good, it settles down and looks peaceful. Pretty soon
though, it begins to sense a relationship between its crying
and its getting taken care of. Crying somehow seems to
make something happen. From the parents' side of things it's
like, "Oh, there he goes again. Darling, would you go and
see what he's crying about?" From the baby's side, it's
more like, "Feel bad . . . cry . . . feel good." So maybe
sometimes the baby even cries when it doesn't really feel
bad, just because crying results in something happening
which makes it feel good. This marks the beginning of the
second petal, control. Control means doing. The infant does
something which results in something happening. He or she
is already embarking on a journey toward doing and control
which will consume the better part of life.

As the child develops and desire and control become
more important and refined aspects of its awareness, a new
realization begins to dawn. There are times when the crying,
or whatever else it is doing, brings results. There are other
times when the results are not forthcoming. Sometimes
crying brings this hovering, smiling, cootchy-cooing object
over the crib. Sometimes it does not. There are things that
can be controlled all the time, and there are things that can't.
With this, the sense of self and other is born. This is the
third petal on awareness. I can control myself, put my hand
here or there or wiggle around, but *that* over *there* I can't
control. I can't get that moon down here so I can feel it. And
that warm wonderful bringer of milk doesn't *always* respond
to my cries. The third petal on the infant's awareness is of
me and you, this and that, subject and object.

By the age of one, the child has had quite a bit of
experience in learning what it can control and what it can't.
It has a pretty good sense of what is self and what is other.
One of the major lessons it's learning is that it has most
control over its own body and mind. Fourth petal. The baby
can move its limbs, stuff things in its mouth, and when it
doesn't get what it wants, it can, in its own mind, pretend
that it did. The sense of "me" is much stronger, and it is
made up of this body and this mind. If the child could think

in these terms, it might introduce itself to us as "me—this body and this mind." Of course it still hasn't formed concepts of body, mind or me, but it has the *sense* of these things. The petals are on.

We parents help fill in the concepts. When the child starts toddling around, we begin to say things like: "Do this!" "Don't do that!" "Why did you do that?" "Watch out!" Words like this emphasize that the child is some *body*, a person, who can do things and control things. The words help to build ideas and concepts.

But these specific words also accomplish something else. They implant the idea of *will*. When we want the child to do something and the child says no, it gets a clear sense that not only is it different from us, but it can also choose to go *against* us. The fifth petal comes into place.

Self-image Now let's try to put all this together and see what has happened to awareness in the midst of it. What the child has been building through this process is a personality. A sense of self. Self-image. By the age of two, the child has a sense that it is what it does, it is its body and mind, it is what it can control, and it is what it wills. To all intents and purposes, that little self-image is made up of will, desire, self/other distinction control, body and mind. All the petals are on.

Throughout childhood, adolescence and even thereafter, these petals get strengthened, clarified and more substantial. So that when you reach adulthood and somebody asks who you are, your answers will almost invariably be in terms of those five factors. "Who are you?" You give your name. "That's just a name. I mean who *are* you?"

"Well, I'm a human being, a woman." (Body/mind)

"I'm an accountant." (Doing; will and control)

"I'm a guy who likes tennis, good friends and poetry." (Desire)

"But I'm not the kind of person who. . ." (Self/other)

What we have here is a self-image, made up of those five petals. But whatever happened to awareness? It got buried in the process somewhere. Basic awareness, which started out at our very core, upon which everything else was built, which enabled us to accomplish everything else; that very awareness has now become totally *subservient* to desire, control, self, body, mind and will. "Why, that's what awareness is *for*," we assume. "We're aware so that we can know what we want and what we don't want; so we can know who we are; so we can decide what to do and do it well; so we can figure things out and keep ourselves under control and be successful at living." The possibility of *just* awareness, awareness which is free of all of that, awareness which exists in its own right, has been relegated to the realms of forgotten memories. Rather than being the base of our existence, awareness is now a slave.

Free awareness Become aware of *any*thing and see if you can keep that awareness free from all the five petals. Can you look at anything without distinguishing it as other and labeling it? Can you watch any part of your body moving without controlling it? Can you sense any thought, image, memory

or perception without being attracted or repelled by some
function of desire? Can you sense any thought without
exerting your will upon it in some way? Can you encounter
any other person without sensing the "other-ness" and
getting involved with attraction or repulsion? Can you ever
be aware of yourself without *doing* something? Not very
often. And not for long.

Now lest we start to give all these petals a bad name,
let's underscore that they are perfectly normal components
of our human be-ing. The problem is that *we've lost
awareness* in among them all. So that most of the time we're
not aware. And when we are, it's almost always accompanied
by one or more of these appendages. It's as if they all were
glued tightly to awareness. It's only very seldom that we get
a glimpse of clean, pure awareness, unfettered and free.

Being lost among these petals is not the only indignity
that awareness must suffer. We also expand large amounts
of energy to keep awareness stifled, restricted and confined.
We call this "Paying Attention."

The Price of Paying Attention

Childness
A very small child, before it learns to be too
discriminating about its sensations, is aware of a lot more
things than you and I usually are. It's crawling around the
floor, sticking things in its mouth and drooling on the rug.
Perhaps its awareness isn't very refined, but it's *open.* It's
open to the feel of the rug on its bare knees, to the sounds of
cars passing and dogs barking outside, to smells wafting
through the house, to the taste of things in its mouth, to the
changing light as the sun goes behind a cloud. All at once!
It's open to all of these sensations and more. And at the *same
time*, it can look for all the world as if it were totally
entranced in one small bug or leaf or toy. It can be interested
in one thing, but still let all sorts of other things into its
consciousness. It doesn't have to shut anything out. It hasn't
yet learned to focus attention. Learning to focus attention is
the beginning of slavery.

Specialness
It won't be long before someone starts telling the child:
"Pay attention!" "Don't look over there while I'm talking to
you!" "Watch where you're going!" Little by little, the child
will learn to narrow its field of vision. Shut things out.
There is nothing wrong with learning to focus attention. The
trouble is that we learn this lesson too well. By the time
we're grown, we are actually uncomfortable, even downright
scared if we aren't homing our attention in on some special
thing. We've been programmed to assume that it's bad or
dangerous or lazy (or at best childish) just to be aware
without being aware *of* anything *special.* Women, I think,
have been spared some of this because of the male
supremacy myths of our society. Little girls are often given
more permission to just sit and sense. Little boys are
expected to be about their business, always doing something.
Later on, young men are expected to be *concentrating* on
whatever is going to get them wherever they want to go. But

paying attention.

Just what is it we're paying? When we think of paying
attention to some specific thing, we often sense our
awareness as a kind of searchlight, beaming in on the object,
illuminating it and making it more clear. This is an almost
completely mistaken view.

One's attention is not at all like a searchlight which is
used to illuminate something. It doesn't really make
anything more clear. In actuality, all we are doing is blocking
out other stimuli. *Almost all the energy that goes into paying
attention is used to block out other stimuli.* Our
manipulation of awareness is not like turning on a
searchlight. It is much more like drawing the curtains or
building a wall to hold everything else out.

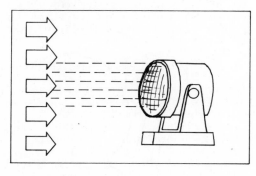

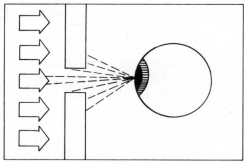

An exercise   Try another experiment. Concentrate very hard upon
this dot. Really try to get it clear and precise:

●

Think about what you're doing. You tend to lean
toward it, narrowing your field of vision so other things
don't come in. You even tend to squint your eyes to further
block out other things. You try to keep other ideas away.
Your body becomes more tense, your breath more constricted.

It's work. But the only *real* focusing that's going on is a minute adjustment of the lens and pupil of your eyes to make allowance for your distance from the paper. All the rest is "curtain drawing." And it doesn't really make the dot more clear. All it does is remove "distractions."

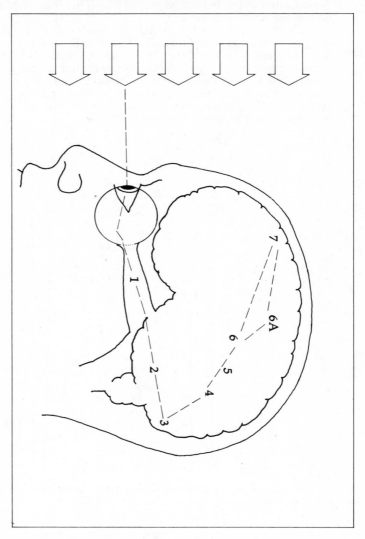

We have a multitude of layers or levels in our central nervous system that are used to *inhibit* or block incoming stimuli. And they all take energy. Use vision as an example. Right now, around you, how many stimuli are there which your eyes don't catch? Millions. And of those your eyes do catch, how many never make it to your awareness? Millions more.

The diagram

In the diagram there is an eyeball extending off the brain on a stalk which is the optic nerve. The arrows are things in our environment which might be seen. Light *comes* from these objects to our eyes. We don't reach out to get them. The light *comes* in. The colors and frequencies to which the eye is sensitive are limited. This and the direction the eye is looking and its lens arrangement already rule out a lot of stimuli. None of that takes much energy. But when the light from the stimulus strikes a visual receptor cell in the back of the eye, the stimulus starts getting conducted electrically, and then we can really start to use blocking energy.

At point number 1 on the diagram, it is possible for the brain to cause the optic nerve to stop conducting the impulse. It may do this if the same impulse has come through again and again so that we're "used" to it. For example, you are continually and repeatedly passing something right in front of your eyes that you are seldom aware of. Your eyelids. Maybe when you were a little baby, the first time you blinked, you might have said, "Hey, what was that?" But by now you're so used to it that you seldom even see it. The reason that you don't see it is because you block it out. You've "learned" that it's more important to pay attention to other things. This happens with all sorts of stimuli. Background sounds, the touch of the ground when you walk, the feeling of the air as you breathe, lots of things. Many of these stimuli never even make it to the brain at all because they've been killed way out there in the nerve. If you think of your sensory nerves as pipelines which carry information from the environment to your consciousness, it is as if your brain, by remote control, had closed a valve on one of those pipelines.

If the stimulus does make it through that valve and on into the brain, it then must pass through a second valve. Point number 2 on the diagram. This one is open if the brain is alert and responsive, but it closes when the brain gets drowsy. This one takes energy too. The brain does a lot of work to shut out stimuli when you're drowsy or asleep. The next point at which the stimulus may be stopped is at the visual cortex (point number 3) where the actual pattern of the stimulus is reproduced in the brain. If the brain is busy doing something else or is shutting off stimuli for some other reason, the image may never get formed. If it *is* formed, there are still more obstacles ahead.

At point 4, the brain sort of looks at the image and makes a preliminary "decision" about whether to let the image pass on into consciousness. This decision, which is formed unconsciously and automatically, is based on whether the image has any meaning or not. Whether or not it makes "sense." For example, you may be familiar with these old diagrams:

Most people don't read the second "the" or "a" because
Expectations their consciousness does not even see them. The eye sees
them, but since they don't really "mean" anything—they
don't fit our expectations—they just don't register in our
consciousness. They are blocked at the meaning checkpoint.
My brother Don is an artist in California. He, like other
sensitive and creative people, is very aware of this kind of
problem. He tries to encourage his students to see what's
around them whether it has "meaning" or not. To help with
this, he once lugged a big lawnmower inside the building and
placed it in the hall. "What did you see on the way in
here?" he asked. People said they saw the walls, the floor,
the door, all the things they'd expected to see. Very few saw
the lawnmower.

After the brain "decides" that the stimulus has
Importance meaning enough to allow through, it then has to figure out
whether the stimulus is *important* enough to pay attention
to. Now we're getting into psychology. Importance is
determined by desire; that first petal on the lotus-flower of
awareness. Something is important if we desire to have it or
if we desire to get away from it. We walk down a busy
sidewalk. Our eyes catch the stimuli of other people's faces,
but we usually don't pay much attention to them, and
therefore don't really *see* them, because they're not very
important to us. But we don't have any trouble seeing faces
that have to do with our desire. We pay attention to the very
beautiful ones and to the mean-hostile-scary ones, because
they've passed the importance test at valve number 5.

Our beleaguered little stimulus still has not made it into
Passports consciousness. It has at least one more filter through which
and customs it must pass. This one is *very* psychological. At the border
crossing between the unconscious and consciousness the
stimulus is stopped and scrutinized by a customs official.
This is a very strict guy who is acting as an agent of our ego,
and he has several questions to ask the stimulus. "Are you
now or have you ever been related to the neurotic hassles of
this mind? Are you going to remind this mind of past
neurotic traumas? Are you going to stimulate some
forbidden sexual or aggressive feelings? Do you symbolize
something this mind is trying to forget? Are you going to
create more problems for this mind in any way?" If the
stimulus can answer "No" to all these questions, it is
allowed to pass on into awareness. But if the answer to any
of them is "Yes," another unconscious decision has to be
made. If the stimulus is going to present some problems and
it isn't terribly important, it is labeled as an undesirable alien
and soundly kicked out. But if it's *very* important, it will be
allowed to pass, with a conditional passport.

The stimulus with a conditional passport usually gets
Laundering sidetracked again before it is allowed to enter consciousness.
It's kind of a de-lousing process. The conditional stimulus is
sort of greasy and unkempt. It needs a laundering. For
example, let's say a somewhat puritanical young gentleman
is walking down a busy street. He's bopping along, not
seeing many of the faces. He passes a grocery store, out of

which is issuing a stream of humanity, all carrying packages.
He doesn't really "see" any of them except those he has to
avoid running into. Then there's this very attractive young
woman who comes out, carrying packages like the rest. Lots
of the old valves open up right away. At the customs station
she gets a conditional passport because there are all sorts of
possibilities for trouble. But she's considered important
enough to let through. At the de-lousing station, all the dirty
little sexual associations that may have gotten attached to her
are scrubbed off and kicked out of the country. (They are
stimuli too.) Then, the sharpness and detail of her
attractiveness are fogged up a bit, and the *packages* she's
carrying are brought into very clear focus. What's seen, after
all of this, is a young woman carrying packages. Helpful and
altruistic as our young subject is, he approaches the woman
with, you guessed it, "Can I help you with the packages?"
"Yes, thank you." Our altruistic friend didn't even *see* all
the other people with packages, old, infirm, or whatever.

The journey   This is just an example, with as many metaphors as
you'd care to mix, of the different kinds of obstacles a
stimulus must overcome on its journey from reality to
consciousness. All in a fraction of a fraction of a second. It
also shows how, by the time a stimulus reaches
consciousness, it may have become so altered that it's almost
unrecognizable. I've listed six valves and filters. There are
countless more. Almost all of them use energy to shut out
stimuli, and it all takes a lot of work. That's why you're tired
after you've been concentrating on something. You've been
tensely and tightly shutting things out. But if you were
relaxed, in your natural, loose, unresisting state, you would
be an open channel. All the stimuli would flow right in.
You'd have lots of things in your consciousness, and you
wouldn't be tired at all. So paying attention, when that
means focusing in on something and shutting out
"distractions," takes a lot of hard work. The answer to our
question about the price of paying attention is now clear.
The fee is energy, and the price is fatigue. Or, in another
sense, the price you pay for paying attention to *one* thing is
your awareness of everything else.

This goes for all stimuli, even those coming from the
mind itself, like memories, impulses and fantasies. We're all
the time shutting them out. In the case of mental stimuli, the
shutting-out process is called *repression*. Some of this may
be necessary, but the way we do it makes the mind tight, in
the same way that our muscles are tight when we contract
them. That's why relaxation is so important if we're going to
do some freeing of awareness. Relaxation means to ease off
some of that constricting, restrictive effort, to open some of
the valves, to be a more open channel.

When awareness is allowed to be free, when relaxation
has created an open channel, perception seems more crystal
clear. There is a feeling of being energized. This is because
some of that tight, constraining energy has been allowed to
free up. One has been closer, for a while, to that natural state
in which the energy of body and mind is used for living, as it

needs to be used, rather than being forced into rigid patterns through clenched teeth, squinting eyes, and grasping hands.

Just being

Why can't we be in this relaxed, open way normally, without meditating? Some people can. But for most of us, it's a different scene. In our growth process with desire, control, will, etc., we have received the message that we can't just live life; we've somehow got to *strive* for it. We can't just be. We've got to work at being. We operate as if we believe that in order to get what we want and avoid what we don't want we must get our hands all over ourselves and always be in charge. Always in control. As if we can't trust our own bodies and minds to live nicely. This is really a totally insane position, of course, because it's our mind that's telling us we can't trust our mind. And it's our mind that's saying, "I have to take over and run this thing very carefully."

From stifling to freeing

We invent all sorts of *parts* of our mind to make this craziness a little easier to swallow. For example, we say, "My mind isn't trustworthy, so *I* have to watch it." That means there's me and there's my mind. Or we say, "Well, my superego or my conscience or my internal parent is too restricting and inhibiting, so *I* always have to try to be more spontaneous." Now there's another part—a conscience that needs to be dealt with. The fact that it's our conscience that's saying we "ought" to deal with our conscience doesn't strike us as ludicrous simply because we're so bound up in the struggle that we haven't the space to see all the insanity that is there. On we go, inventing new parts of ourselves for other parts of ourselves to deal with and watch out for. Then, almost every time we get some awareness, we immediately pull it into our tight little battle with ourselves and stifle it. It is for us then, the meddlers with being, that some practice-in-pretending to free awareness may be helpful.

Growth into Spiritual Longing

From unity to separation

A child is born in unity and grows up into separation. In modern society this is seen as the admirable way. By adulthood the individual is expected to have a solid image of self, a sense of what he or she wants out of life, and the knowledge of how to get it. Ego is expected to be strong, and identity is supposed to be autonomous and stable.

This is a big order. It is not so difficult to learn things. But to acquire the expected degree of personality solidity, a young person must wind up freezing himself or herself. The world must be made rigid, and this is a terrible price to pay for adulthood. Being must be sacrificed for doing, and growth must be stifled in favor of building.

This may well be the natural state of affairs for modern man or woman. We certainly seem to have little choice about it. In this society the hope of growing up freely and remaining at one during the process is very idealistic. But if this is the natural state of affairs, perhaps it is not so awful. There is, after all, a great beauty in seeing the one beginning whole, fragmenting into individual sparkles which dance out their little lives, finally to merge into one again. There could be peace in this.

The trouble is not in the process of individuation. The trouble is more in the fact that we too often lock off and become frozen in the individualized state. We assume that socially acceptable adulthood is the end; that there is no going beyond autonomy. We blindly believe that the ultimate goal of life is to master ourselves as good, healthy, well-*adjusted*, happy and independent adults.

Maturity Some years ago Harry Stack Sullivan described what he thought to be a stage of growth beyond adulthood. He called it *maturity*. He said it was characterized by love rather than self-interest. He also said only a few people make it into this stage of growth.

Harry Stack Sullivan was not so unusual in having this vision. Every mind, great and small, contains a memory of union and a longing for reunion. And a small bare hope that that reunion might happen in the course of living. This vision may not be clearly specified, and it may not be given much credence in the world of today. Often it is stifled, labeled as crazy, or otherwise buried beneath the rigidity of adulthood. But still it is there. And in moments however brief, it is seen.

Moments of decision When the vision is seen, it becomes a longing, which in turn becomes a nagging. And the nagging forces one into a decision. Whether to allow the nagging to create cracks in one's rigidity or by brute force to bury it again. There are several points in life when this decision simply must be made.

One is in early childhood, around kindergarten-age, when self-image is brand-new and union is still a fresh memory. Another is in adolescence, when "Who am I?" assumes a dramatically ultimate importance. Another is at the beginning of parenting or vocation, where there is a sense of "O.K., here I am, set and committed and ready to go. I do hope it goes well." Still another occurs in mid-life, when the wisdom finally dawns that there is no way under heaven of actualizing all one's fantasies. And then there is older age, when one's children are grown, retirement becomes a reality, and death lies over the next few hills.

Each of these are moments of pause. They are places for re-evaluation. Windows into the union of the past and the reunion of the future. At any one of these points, if the rigidity of who-I-am is allowed to crack a bit, a true spiritual quest may begin. A quest for being who one already most really is. The active search for God.

An example As an example, look at what might happen to a typical upper middle class American male.

At first he is pictured as a young-man-who-knows-where-he's-going. He stands tall and walks with confidence. Eyes straight ahead. His ego (self-image, identity) is solid, and it is securely embedded in the back of his head.

Suddenly he happens upon a flower. A lily of the field.

Something which in its unassuming innocence brings him
into a moment of realizing one-ness. For that brief instant,
he can do nothing but stand and see. And his ego, for that
little speck of time, is gone.

Immediately thereafter he is troubled. His ego, now a
little lopsided and insecure, is feeling threatened. But the
man's basic nature is calling him back to the flower. At first
perplexed, he soon begins to experience true anxiety. The
dilemma is simple. "Do I sacrifice my ego in order to live, or
do I simply pretend to live in order to protect my ego?"

At this point he will act. His anxiety will force him to
move, and he can go one of three directions. If he takes
direction number 1, he has chosen to have his cake and eat it
too. He tries to stay with the flower and at the same time
cling to his own ego. And thus he will become insane.
Psychotic. A man is coming for him with a net, because
union and individual ego can co-exist only in a world of
delusion.

Or he may take direction number 2. Which is perhaps
the most common among successful American males of
today. He runs like hell. He gets away from the flower just
as fast as he can. Back to the world of doing,
accomplishment and self-determination. Back to where he
may feel alienated, but at least he's some*body*. Back to nurse
his ego's wounds.

Or he may choose direction number 3. A spiritual path.
In one way or another he stays with a sense of the flower,
reaching out to it. And he lets his own ego be risked in the
process. He is willing, perhaps even desiring to have his ego
become less important and less secure.

Whichever path he chooses, there is both trouble and
hope ahead. And there undoubtedly will be many
convolutions and blind allies in his journey. In path number
1, the convolutions include psychotherapy, self-fixing,
labeling himself as sick, dulling awareness with drugs or
defenses, and perhaps most dangerous of all, getting well.

In path numbr 2, he will be trapped by success and
achievement. Mastery of himself. Financial security.
Corporate responsibility. And the ice-age of conformity.

The third path, the spiritual quest, is not at all any
better. Here he will be caught by his own sense of holiness.
By identifying himself as a spiritual person. By collecting
mystical experiences. And by defining himself away from the
secular world. Perhaps by seeing himself as better than
others. Every spiritual discipline will have a devil in it for
him saying, "Come on, do this, and if you succeed you will
be better than you were before."

Somehow within all the convolutions of all the paths,
grace lends a hand. The natural process of things evolves as
it evolves. God's will is done. The karmic chain unfolds. Our
young man, now perhaps quite old, may have grown. To
some extent he may have grown into becoming smaller.
Achievement just might have moved toward acceptance.

Suffering and rage toward compassion. Individualism could 158
have been tempered by the realization of union. And
awareness may be a little more free. And being more real.

All of this is a stereotyped and highly conceptualized
A summary description of what in reality is the infinitely variable
process of living. Hopefully it does not recommend a course
to follow. But it does say three things to me.

One is that there is nothing to be achieved.

The second is that we shall try to achieve it
nonetheless.

And the third is that this is precisely
the way things should be.

The Forms of Meditation

There are innumerable kinds of meditation. But they all
What's share, at one time or another, the common denominator of
common being aware of awareness. Being aware *that* you are aware.
We are nearly always aware of things, but only seldom do
we sense that awareness directly. Whatever form of
meditation one practices, and for whatever ends, one does
confront the fact that one is aware. The same is true of
prayer.

At the present time, I cannot distinguish between
prayer and meditation. I once did see prayer as a sort of
talking relationship, in which there was a clear distinction
between the me-self and the other-God. But even in that
One life noisy sort of prayer, there is a sense of being aware. And
that sense is greatly amplified when prayer becomes more
quiet, more listening, more receptive and more
contemplative.

In the western Christian spiritual tradition, meditation
is most closely associated with what is called *contemplative
prayer*. In this tradition, contemplation does not mean
thinking *about* something. It is rather that quiet open
receptivity in which one is just being. People have made up
various hierarchies of prayer, ranging from concentration to
meditation and to comtemplation. I will not go into these
here, for they are well described elsewhere and I have some
trouble ranking one state of consciousness above another. It
tends to make too much of a thing of awareness. But it is
worthwhile to realize that prayer and meditation are basically
the same. As a matter of fact, to whatever degree one is able
to give up and just be, it is to that degree that one's entire
life is prayer.

Some kinds of meditation help awareness be free,
Kinds of usually because of their simplicity. Others are likely to trap
meditation awareness more than ever. Usually because of their
complexity. But whatever form is practiced, it is probably
the attitude of the meditator which will make the most
difference. If you see awareness as an object to be
manipulated, something to be "altered," something to
master, then you will bury it no matter what you do. On the
other hand, if you approach awareness with awe, if the
wonder of it transcends all your thoughts and words, then it

is likely to be flying free whether you meditate formally or
not. Meditation, no matter what else it may be, cannot be a
means to an end. Not if it is to allow freedom for being. The
paradox of this statement must simply be accepted. There is
no way around it. The purpose of meditation is just to be.
But in order for just being to happen, there can be no
purpose.

A scheme Before the paradoxes become too thick, it might be
helpful to organize some different kinds of meditation in the
form of an outline. There are so many kinds around today
that it can all be very confusing. Perhaps this little outline
will lend a sense of order, for whatever that may be worth.

Meditation

I. **Spontaneous**
II. **Intentional**
    A. **Informal**
    B. **Formal**
        1. **The Hard Push Way**
        2. **The Trance-and-Travel Way**
        3. **The Open Way**

Spontaneous meditation is something we have all
experienced. It's when awareness of being just happens.
When just being just happens. Walking through the woods
and being "caught" by the sounds and smells and
atmosphere. Noticing a sunset, hearing a morning bird.
Being pregnant and feeling the life inside, seeing Christmas
in the eyes of a child. Swept up by a symphony, captured by
a poem, lost in the ecstasy of love. Moments when existence
is truly savored, without any thinking about it and without
even any sense of you being there savoring it. Moments of
fully, freely, naturally wide-awake being.

How different are these moments of being lost in
awareness from other moments when awareness is lost in
doing something. Sometimes we confuse these two kinds of
losing. We seek to lose ourselves in a good book, a television
program, a sport or a hobby. But though these activities
usually help free us from worry, planning and evaluation,
it is awareness which is lost in them. They are like narcotics,
killing awareness in order to provide relief from discomfort.
How different this is from the spontaneous moments when
"we" are lost and awareness springs up bright and clear.
Again, it is not the activity itself which makes the difference.
It is whether awareness is stifled or free. Spontaneous
meditation is when awareness breaks free, without any
trying. Without any intent. Nothing is stifled and nothing
is denied. Being is full and complete, and awareness is sharp
and clear.

In those moments, one doesn't think about it. There is
no thought of "My, isn't this beautiful." That kind of
thinking comes a little while *after* the moment, and that kind
of thinking usually destroys the moment. As soon as we
recognize how marvelous the moment is, we try to grasp it;

prolong it. In so doing, we lose it, and awareness is trapped
again.

Intentional meditation is just what it says. It's willful.
It's done with conscious intent. Most people have also
experienced intentional meditation, though perhaps not
recognizing it as such. Whenever one looks inside, sensing
the qualities of awareness for some purpose, intentional
meditation happens. The purpose could be anything.
Suddenly realizing you've become tense or worried or sad,
you stop and take stock of things. Seeing what's going on in
the mind. Or in experiencing a happy feeling, some joy or
satisfaction, intentionally stopping to savor it. Or having
just experienced the sweetness of spontaneous meditation,
trying to keep it. Or trying to recreate it. Or analyzing one's
self. Intentional meditation usually traps awareness rather
than frees it. Because we're trying to accomplish something,
awareness gets lost amid all the effort and doing. In order to
avoid this, one must learn something about relaxing, opening
and allowing. This is where practice comes in.

There are two kinds of intentional meditation. One is
where some special time is set aside for practice. This is
formal meditation. It's what usually comes to mind when
one thinks of *meditating;* sitting in a cave or in your living
room, concentrating, contemplating, or openly experiencing
awareness. TM, yoga, contemplative prayer, Zazen, the
silence of Quaker meetings are all ways of formal
meditation.

Informal meditation takes place during the rest of life,
when there isn't any special time set aside for meditation. It
happens casually, almost spontaneously, without much
effort. Informal meditation means to *watch.* To tune in to
your awareness in the midst of whatever is going on. To
remember life in the middle of living. It takes only a little
nudge. Walking down the street, it occurs, "Here I am."
Working at the office or at home, you realize "I'm being
here right now," and you watch. Just a little conscious
attempt to be aware during all the things you do.

Return for a moment to *formal meditation.* Whatever
technique is used for formal meditation, the attitude of the
meditator can go one of three ways.

The first way I have chosen to call the "hard-push
Hard-push way." Here one uses great effort to center attention on one
way subject or thought and to block out any other thoughts or
sensations. It is very possible for the hard-push way
ultimately to result in freer awareness, but the process
involves great mind manipulation and unless done "just
right" it encourages repression. Without very competent
guidance it can be dangerous.

The second way may not involve so much effort, but
Trance-and- what it does instead is encourage fantasy "trips" away from
travel way clear present reality. I have chosen to call this the "trance-
and-travel way" because it fosters a sense of altered
consciousness and a feeling of going "off" somewhere. This
way also involves significant manipulation of the mind, and
encourages a disassociation of consciousness from
sensations.

Open way

The third way, or "open way," involves great gentleness rather than great effort. It moves toward absence of mind-manipulation. It moves toward a natural, spontaneous state in which awareness is bright and clear, receptive to everything in the here and now.

It is clear from the text of this book and from the above descriptions that my bias lies rather dramatically in the direction of the open way. Though it appears that each of the ways of formal meditation have been "helpful" to different people in different ways, I should like to discuss my perception of them at somewhat greater length.

Burning out

The open approach to meditation described in this book may seem very different from many other traditions. The hard-push approaches of meditation and concentration say you should put all the energy you can into keeping your attention on one thing, while the open approach is to use as little effort as possible. With the one tradition control and will are pushed to their maximum. In the other is total permissiveness. Any two things which are as opposite as that have to be the same at core. And they are, really. The high-powered approach is ultimately geared toward breaking through the trying, the struggling and the control of attention by utilizing these forces so completely that they finally burn out and fall apart. The Zen student may struggle for years, using every bit of available energy to understand something that can't be understood, such as "What is the sound of one hand clapping?" Until, at some point, he or she burns out, the fuses blow, the circuits overload, and giving up is the only thing left. Then awareness comes flying up like the Phoenix from the ashes. In the open way, it's more like gently incubating an egg until the chick hatches itself. Either way, the bird winds up free. Hopefully.

The hard-push way has consistently caused some not-so-good things to happen in my experience. One is that I get exhausted with it. It seems I am left with less energy for daily living. And I tend to get funky and irritable after a meditation in which I've been trying hard. This occurs for a couple of reasons. First, I have just spent a lot of energy repressing and shutting out stimuli, and my mind is bound to rebel. Second, I tend to feel that if I put so much effort into meditation I ought to "get" something for it—like maybe enlightened. And when I find I'm not, I feel a bit disgruntled.

Often after a hard-push meditation I feel as if I am in a daze rather than sharp and clear. That's because for me the hard-push way encourages "trance-and-travel" experiences. It encourages a dis-association between consciousness and perceptions, and one feels as if one has been "off" somewhere away from the here and now. This is where consciousness truly becomes "altered," and I'm not at all convinced of the value of this.

The trance-and-travel way is like a kind of self-hypnosis. It puts one into a form of trance or encourages vivid fantasy trips. It has become quite popular of late in human-potential group work when it is associated with music or with special instructions to picture yourself in certain situations where certain events happen to you. The old Christian form of visual prayer in which one visualizes a Bible story and participates in it is also a trance-and-travel meditation. So are meditations assisted by psychedelic drugs, sensory deprivation, and sometimes biofeedback. The psychics and mediums of spiritualism are often familiar with trance-and-travel meditations, and frequently feel that their trances put them in touch with different planes or levels of consciousness in which they have very valuable experiences.

There are in fact many different states of consciousness. One is your "normal" waking state. Another is sleep. Still another is dreaming. Many others occur spontaneously in almost any kind of meditation. Hypnosis, trances and various kinds of reveries produce still more. With all these possibilities for exploring and altering consciousness, it is easy to understand the popularity of trance-and-travel approaches. It can be very interesting and seductive. And powerful.

Trips One begins to see the mind as a great new frontier, a vast uncharted territory filled with adventure and excitement. You begin to feel like a Christopher Columbus sailing bravely into unknown seas. It is now possible to find many books filled with maps of these "territories" of consciousness, describing all the stages and planes, levels and places one can "go" to. There's nothing inherently wrong with any of this, but it is very easily abused. One abuse is that these possibilities present ever more opportunity for self-alteration and self-manipulation. If this is one's attitude, there will be nothing but an unending search for fulfillment, a continuous collection of complicated experiences which take one further and further away from the simple reality of things-as-they-are.

Another abuse is that people often find themselves "going" to other planes of consciousness in order to escape from this one. And this also is bound for despair, because sooner or later one always winds up back here, because this is where you always really are and always will be. Whatever is happening in this very moment is what you've been given to work with and suffer from and appreciate. There's nothing more and nothing less. You are who you are, where you are, when you are, and that's all there is to it.

Your experience may be different from mine, but I experimented with all sorts of "altered" states of consciousness; with biofeedback and psychedelics, hypnosis and fantasy trips, sensory deprivation and hyperventilation, and I got bored. At the time the experiences seemed wondrous, inexplicable, beautiful. Some were terrifying or tragically sad. But after a while I got bored. You can walk around Disneyland eating hot dogs and being entertained for a long time. But after a while it all kind of blurs together, and you feel a little stuffy-full, and you begin to get this hankering to go home. Even if you have not filled your insatiable appetite for entertainment, they're bound to close the gates and kick you out sometime. You always have to 163 come "back," whether you want to or not.

If you find yourself returning to the "real" world before you're ready, you may get pretty depressed. That's what they mean when they talk about "coming down from a spiritual high." Somehow it seems that "there" is better, more colorful, more exciting, than "here." But here is where you always wind up. After enough of this bruising, a few fortunate souls seem to wake up to the fact that a clump of earth or a blade of grass or anything else that *is right here right now* is far more incredibly wonderful and miraculous than anything one could encounter in the wildest of mind-trips. And then there is hope for just being. There's no place like home. And there's no place *but* home.

It may be that you think "home" is not a very nice place to be. It may be filled with worry or pain or ugliness. If that's the case, you may want to skip the country when you alter your consciousness. You will probably want to go further and further out on your "trips." And perhaps you'll hope that sometime you may never come back. But it won't work. They keep closing the gates and tossing you back. As painful as that may be, it's really a blessing. Because eventually you have to give up. And when you do, you'll recognize that the only thing left is here and now. And then it may be possible to begin seeing here and now. And it will all open up. There will be some space in the midst of you and your life and your pain. Not the kind of space that takes you away, but the kind of space which lets you see.

Finally, it has been my experience that both hard-push and trance-and-travel ways of meditation tend to make me feel more important, that what I'm doing is really *significant*, so that I take myself very seriously. I tend to feel very special about myself and my meditation and my spiritual growth. And it all starts to get heavy. All the lightness and open awareness become buried under my clinging and clutching. And a bigger ego like this is something I most assuredly do not need.

The open way, I think, is much safer. I've never seen any people psychologically hurt by letting themselves be who they are. Or by opening their eyes. It is healing rather than hurt which takes place in this kind of atmosphere. The hurts come when we stifle awareness, pick at ourselves and push too hard. And when we get to feeling very important. It doesn't matter whether you feel important because you're so good or because you're so bad or because you're hurting so much or because you're so unusual. Self-importance is self-importance no matter what its quality or cause. And self-importance is asking for trouble.

If you should wish to experiment with hard-push or trance-and-travel ways of meditation, or if you find yourself wanting to turn some of the exercises in this book into effortful pieces of work, I would strongly suggest you seek out some very competent guidance. How you decide what is competent and what is not I shall leave, gratefully, in your hands.

The American way

Perhaps no aspect of meditation so strikes against the backbone of Americanism as passivity. Being passive, even thinking about being passive, is enough to make our red blood curdle. If we are inhibited, we are taught that we ought to express our feelings. If we are humble, we are taught to be assertive. We make jokes about how alien passivity is to us. We laugh at the alleged Zen instruction, "Don't just do something; sit there." But our laughter is not in the nature of a hearty guffaw. It is more like a cynical and slightly anxious snicker. We are a culture of doers, a civilization built on accomplishment, standing up for our rights, fighting for liberty, and above all growing and getting somewhere.

Even for that generation of do-gooders of which I am a part—the civil rights and anti-war marchers, the peace wagers and brotherly lovers—even for us, the association of passivity with meditation releases a swarm of "bad vibes." We saw Maharishi Mahesh Yogi and Guru Mahara-ji flying half-way around the world to bring us peace of mind from India, and we laughed with bitterness. "How come," we'd say, "if your spirituality is so great, that so many people are starving in your own land?" "And how can you come here and tell *us* to sit on our behinds for twenty minutes twice a day when our own countrymen are starving and killing each other in the streets and not getting educated and being oppressed?" The eastern missionaries would have answers for us, but either the answers had meaning only if we knew the language of mysticism, or we didn't want to hear.

Our assumption that meditation means passivity caused us to forget about all the meditating spiritual giants who did get very involved in doing good for their fellow humans. Like Mahatma Gandhi and Jesus Christ and the Buddhist monks who died in Vietnam and the Catholic saints who gave more energy to service than we could ever dream of giving. And we also tended to forget the far-more-than-twenty-minutes-twice-a-day we spend sitting on our behinds anyway, "doing" things like watching television, reading, gossiping and yelling at umpires. None of these considerations really entered our minds, because we were watching these jokers from the east unabashedly telling us not only that just sitting there was all right, but that it was the way to a better world.

Three reasons

Sitting still, doing nothing, meditating in the midst of a frantic world is a red flag to our social consciousness. There are at least three reasons for this attitude. One is reality. We are correct in recognizing that the world continuously cries out for something to be done and that we *must* act in constructive ways if we are to be a part of it. And it is also correct to recognize that some people have used meditation as a way of escaping from the responsibilities and agonies of living.

The second reason has to do with our own mental

treachery. We can never do enough for our fellow humans anyway, and we are bound to carry some guilt about the pain of the world no matter what we do. So when some guy comes along and sounds like he's saying "It's fine to sit and do nothing," that's *not* what we want to hear. We don't want to learn how to do more nothing. We want to learn how to do more *something*. Something constructive. Besides that, our minds rebel against the very idea of getting quiet. They're afraid they'll cease to exist if they stop making noise. So they want to attack anyone who says, "Get quiet." They think they're fighting for their lives.

Both these reasons make sense, and are quite understandable. But the third reason for our upset about passivity and meditation is really quite sad. It is because we have grossly *misunderstood*. The fact is, there is nothing whatsoever about meditation that says you need to be passive. As a matter of fact, the goal of meditation is to be most fully and appropriately active; to be completely and vibrantly alive every single moment. To do what needs to be done in the world. To bite into life and chew it and digest it completely. To immerse yourself in living and to burn with all the energy of your being. There is no passivity here at all.

An explanation Some explanation is needed? When I say "let yourself be," I don't mean sit and do nothing. That would not be letting yourself be. That would be making yourself do nothing. If you *really* let yourself be, you'd allow your laziness to be, but you'd also let your desire to do something be. Your laziness and your desire to do something will cancel each other out if you keep your grubby hands off them, and then you'll be free to do what needs to be done. You may think that letting your laziness and your need to do something cancel each other out would leave you nothing to do. That's because you feel you cannot act without *desire*. But desire doesn't have to be involved at all. Without so much pulling of desire one way and the other, you'd be free to do what *needs* to be done. Not necessarily what you *want* to do, or what you think you *ought* to do, but simply what needs to be done. Super freedom. It's hard to get our heads around this one. The problem is that we don't trust ourselves to do what needs to be done. If I say, "Let go," which means to get out of the driver's seat of your bulldozer, you don't trust that you'd do the right thing. "I might do something really awful!" Remember though, I'm not saying to kill your conscience or your superego or your morality. I'm saying keep your grubby hands off them and let them do their thing. They'll take care of your ugly bestial Id impulses. *You* don't have to. And you don't have to lose your awareness in the struggle.

An example As an example, let's say your unconscious mind is producing a really ugly, repulsive sexual impulse and your conscience gets wind of it. You sense this happening. Inside your head it might sound like, "Hmmm, I'd really like to. . . ." "Now wait a minute. That's an awful idea." "But I'd really like to. . . ."

Conscience or Morality,
Getting Ready
To Do Battle

Ugly Impulse

Bubbles
in a Seething
Cauldron of Nastiness

Id.

Your Mind

What usually happens is that as soon as we become aware of the impending struggle, we have to mess with it. Since we don't trust our minds to handle the problem, we throw our awareness into the middle of the fray. Somehow, we're convinced that this will make things come out better.

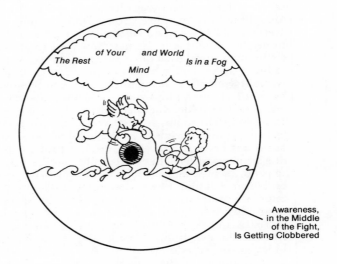

The Rest   of Your   and World
Mind   Is in a Fog

Awareness,
in the Middle
of the Fight,
Is Getting Clobbered

But in a meditative way, or in a consciousness-freeing way, your awareness is not enmeshed in the battle. The battle goes on, with all the control and strength and struggle necessary. Awareness sees it all, and at the same time it can see the rest of your mind and world right then. There is some *space* in the midst of it all.

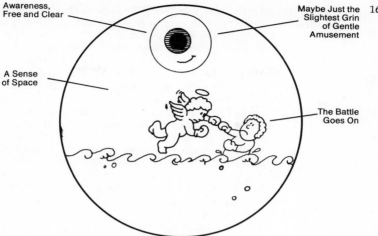

Fear　　How does the fight come out? Who wins, the conscience or the ugly impulse? Well, that's the risk. That's where the fear comes in. Our fantasy is that if we take our hands off ourselves, even for a moment, we'll turn into raving maniacs or slovenly vegetables. Or we'll get abused by others in the world around us. So we've always got to be enmeshing our awareness in an attempt to increase control, grabbing the steering wheel for dear life in our sweaty palms, using every bit of consciousness to be *on guard*. That's why we've come to contract the phrase "Be aware" into the word "Beware." What I'm suggesting is not to kill or stifle your need to control in any way. Just step back from it a bit and let it be. Is there any reason it has to capture your awareness? Don't kill anything in yourself—just get back and watch it a little. Control what you need to. Just begin to find out that your consciousness does *not* have to be kidnapped by that controlling. Your consciousness can be free, alive and well right here and now while all of your controlling takes place. Ask yourself, "If all I have to work with is my mind, of what value is it to glue my awareness to the problem so that the rest of life is shut out while the fight is going on?" Think about the conscience struggling with the ugly impulse. Is it really going to make the battle come out any better if your awareness is captured by the battle? Isn't it possible that it would be better to have your awareness free so that you could sense a lot of other things as *well* as the battle?

Bad guys　　At this point, you could reasonably say, "That may be all right for you and me who have strong consciences and good impulse control. Maybe it's true that we could let our minds work it out and we'd come out all right. But what about 'those people' like criminals and junkies and bad guys who don't have self-control? What happens if *they* let themselves be?" And you might add, in a whisper, "And to be perfectly honest, I'm not so sure about you and me." I've spent four recent years working with people who have immersed themselves in crimes and impulse-gratifications of the most atrocious kinds. The shocker is that they stifle and control themselves as much as or more than you and I do. They kill their awareness just as you and I do, though sometimes they're more direct and forthright about it. And they most certainly do *not* let themselves be. They're into getting their grubby hands on themselves maybe even more than you and I. They just arrange things differently.

Where you or I might spend most of our controlling energy in trying to get along with society and keep our impulses quiet and our consciences appeased, *they* spend incredible amounts of controlling energy trying *not* to get along with society, and attempting to keep their *consciences* quiet and their *impulses* appeased. And they most certainly *do* have consciences. Great big painful ones. They may not act as if they have consciences, just as you or I may not act as if we have dirty crummy impulses, but their consciences are alive and well and continually squawking because they're being sat upon.

I truly believe that if the "criminal" or the "psychopath" could really let himself or herself be, he or she wouldn't be a "criminal" or "psychopath" anymore. I've seen it happen. But the idea of letting one's self be is as scary to "them" as it is to "us." Because the question always arises, "Well, then, what *would* I be?" Whether you're a hardened criminal or a straight arrow, letting yourself be means easing your grip on your *ideas* about your identity. And that is scary for all of us. For some insane reason, we're really afraid to be what we are instead of what we think we are. Even if what we are is very beautiful.

So it makes sense to be worried about what meditation will do to your sense of identity. It may very well get you less and less clear as to precisely who or what you are. But it's not worth it to worry more than you absolutely have to about meditation turning you into a beast or a vegetable. Not unless you start growing fangs or sprouting foliage.

At the risk of being disgustingly redundant, let me say again that letting go does not mean killing your controls. What it does mean is to let go of your consciousness, free it, liberate it so that it can be fully aware, right now, while all the controlling and doing go on. Even with that said, the idea of letting go remains frightening. There's a wonderful series of stories and jokes about letting go, which emphasizes the universality of that fear. It's one of those stories that can be found in many different spiritual traditions.

A Zen story   In Zen, the story is not so much a joke as a koan. As the story goes, a Zen master is walking along a cliff and falls off, catching himself on a branch by his teeth. He's hanging there by his teeth, thinking whatever Zen masters think in such situations, when a student comes by and asks, "What is the meaning of life?" Or "What is Buddha nature?" Or some equally dumb question. The problem of the koan is this: What does the master do? If he does not answer, he will not have done his masterly duty in responding to the student. If he does, he'll surely fall to his death. That's the

Then there's an ancient story that has, I think, both
Christian and Islamic origins. A man is walking along a cliff
and falls off, catching himself on a branch, this time with his
hands. (I always wondered why the Zen master couldn't use
his hands. Is that the answer to the koan?) Anyway, the
guy is hanging there and he's pleading to God, "Is there
anyone up there? Please help me!" God answers, through
the clouds, "Trust me. Let go." Then it's a test of faith, and
there the story ends, although our fantasies are bound to
take it further.

A Christian and Islamic story

One of these fantasies is probably responsible for a
modern American version of the story. This version has
taken on a very racist, or at least a very bigoted aroma. I've
heard it told in reference to at least three different racial and
ethnic groups. Let's say there's this guy from Upper
Grumpia and he's walking along a cliff, falls off, grabs the
branch, and pleads, "Is there anyone up there? Help me!"
God answers, true to form, "Trust me. Let go." The guy
does, and immediately falls to his death on the rocks below.
God speaks again, through the clouds, "That'll teach you,
you stupid Grumpian."

Americana

Finally (we're getting to the end now), there's one that
was told to me by an Eastern Orthodox priest who said it
was a Jewish man walking along the cliff. Why Jewish I'm
not sure, except that it's O.K. to label him as something
because he's the only hero in all these stories who really has
a sensible approach to the thing. He's walking along the
cliff and falls off, like the others, and grabs the branch and
pleads to God, "Is there anyone up there? Help me!" God,
who must now be sounding like a broken record, says,
"Trust me. Let go." The guy thinks for a minute and then,
eyes uplifted to the sky, says, "Is there anyone else up
there?"

Orthodox-Jewish story

It doesn't matter what culture you come from or what
tradition you may find yourself in. There's always anxiety
when we think about letting go. The analogy of falling off a
cliff is a good one to describe our feelings about letting go. It
feels aimless. It feels passive. Our awareness is so used to
getting hooked into all the controlling and doing that if we
think about freeing it, it sometimes feels as though we
wouldn't *have* any awareness. And that feels like death.
Hitting the rocks below. We don't trust that the controlling
and doing can go on superbly without having to hijack our
awareness; that our awareness can be broad enough and
panoramic enough to *see* the controlling, the doing, and
everything else that's happening right now without getting
kidnapped. The truth is, and the paradox is, that you only
really get actively involved when you've created some space
between awareness and doing, so that awareness is free to
see it *all*.

Whatever culture

We've looked at free awareness watching our
conscience control an ugly impulse. Before we conclude this
discussion of passivity and letting go, let's look at awareness
watching *doing*.

Doing

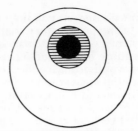

Seeing All the Wonderfulness and Ugliness
of the World:

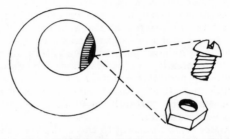

Seeing Something That Needs To Be Done:

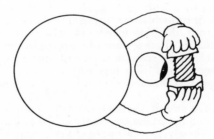

Usually, Our Awareness Gets Glued to the Doing:

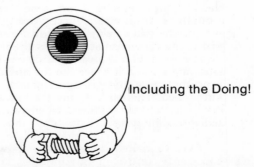

Including the Doing!

In a Meditative Way, All the Wonderfulness
and Ugliness of the World Can Be Seen,

**Meditation
for**

I hope all this discussion will help with an understanding of some of our *mis*understandings about passivity and letting be. But I don't expect it to still your fears. If we didn't fear the consequences of making space between awareness and doing, there'd be no need to meditate. That's what meditation is for. It is an experiential testing ground. In meditation you repeatedly let go a little, create some space, and see what happens. It's the laboratory where you gradually discover that when you take your hands off yourself and let yourself be, you're O.K. Meditation can be the way you find out for yourself. Nobody in his or her right mind would ask you or me to just drop all our doubts and start trusting.

**The
Message
of Love**

Well, that's not completely true. I think the message of the Christian Gospel and of the Sufi Path of Love and of certain other faiths is that you can do that. That you are O.K. as you are. You are loved, accepted, forgiven without having to do anything special to yourself. All you have to do is accept that, make the "leap of faith" and start living. If you can do that, or if you have, then none of this will be a problem, and your meditations will be celebration, thanksgiving and communion. And rightly so. If you haven't been able to do that, meditation can be your laboratory. If you need proof, meditation can be where you collect your evidence. In the laboratory you need accept nothing without first-hand knowledge. There, it's building trust rather than leaping to faith.

In ending this discussion, there is one more story to tell about a man falling off a cliff. This story is attributed to Buddha himself, and though it now occurs in many forms, it purports to describe Buddha's prescription for the basic attitude one should have toward one's life.

A man was walking through a bright green forest when he heard a twig snap behind him. Turning, he saw the red eyes of a huge tiger. He began to run. The tiger followed. Later, almost out of breath, the man looked back and saw that now there were *two* tigers chasing him. Their deep yellow bodies were immense as they charged after him. He ran until he was exhausted and found himself at the edge of a cliff. There was no other way of escape. He jumped off. Halfway down, his left hand caught a small branch, and he hung there. Looking up, he could see the tigers' faces leering at him. Looking down, far below, he saw deep blue water, in which floated an entire battalion of green crocodiles, their mouths wide open to receive him. Then his weight began to cause the branch to break. In the midst of this, his eyes happened to fall upon the face of the cliff in front of him. There, in a tiny rock crevice, grew three bright red berries. With his free hand he plucked them and ate them. How delicious they were!

Questions To Ask Your "Self"

It is tempting to want to know why one meditates, or

why one is going about trying to be who one already is. To look for results, or movement towards a goal. Something to be achieved.

It is perhaps better to be without these kinds of concepts, but there is some danger in having no idea at all about what one is doing. The prime danger is that one will simply go seeking after experience, collecting spiritual "highs" and adding to one's already crammed larder of "stuff."

The realm of the question
Somewhere in between aimless wandering and zealous achievement lies the realm of the question. It is in the question, rather than in the statement, that wisdom lies. Therefore rather than attempting to provide a rationale for your practices-in-pretending-to-be, I will suggest a number of questions for you to ask yourself as time goes along. The answers will never be as important as the process of your asking the questions. Move into the questions, deeply, completely. Let them hang around with you. Keep aware of them. Just keep wondering.

What is your heritage? In religion, in being, in life itself? You may wish to move into this by drawing a picture of the history of your being, from birth until now. Perhaps make it in the form of a line-graph, reflecting the ups and downs and ins and outs. Or describe the times awareness was most open and clear, and most clouded and dull. What have been the most meaningful experiences of your life? Were they things you accomplished, or things which happened, or both? What events, encounters, people, and history have impacted most upon the quality of your being? What kinds of blocks and resistances has your heritage contributed to your awareness?

What is the nature of your spirit? What does life mean to you in the largest sense? What is the real relationship between "your" consciousness and that of other people? Are there times when you feel at one? At one with what? Who is God to you? What is God to you? Relationship or infusion, awe or love? What is prayer to you? Where do your values, your senses of rightness and wrongness come from? How important are you to you? What is the significance of your image of yourself? What is the meaning, the true meaning, of space? of time? of creation?

What is your being in relation to others? What is love for you and for others? What is the true meaning of compassion? What is the role you play in responding to the needs of other human beings; and is it because you should, or because you will feel good, or is it because something needs to be done? What is the relationship between being and social justice, politics, government, civilization? Is there bonding between you and others? Do you have a sense of responsibility to others? What is this sense? What is the space between you and other people? How distant? What makes it up?

Who are you? Do you have a relationship with yourself? Do you like or dislike yourself? How important are you to you? Inside your mind, inside your body, behind your soul, where are *you?* What is your death to you? Does it happen a long time from now? What is the space between you and what you perceive? What parts of you could you do without and still be you?

How do you feel? Not whether you feel good or bad, but *how*, in what way do you feel? What are feelings? What do they do with you and what do you do with them? What is the weight of a feeling? What is important in your feelings? What is lasting? Watch one feeling and see how long it stays. What is feeling love, or hate? Does it matter whether you pay attention to a feeling or not?

What do you think? And how? Where are the origins of your thoughts? How long do they last? What is the space between them and you? What is a memory, what is a hope? Is there a difference? Where do you go when you sleep? When you dream? Who is having the thoughts in a dream? Do you control your thoughts? Who is controlling whom?

There are many other questions. Any time you make a distinction between this and that, between me and it, you can ask a question. And it might be wise to do so.

There is often a feeling, with questions such as these, of some repulsion and disgust. "That's like asking how many angels can dance on the head of a pin. Of what possible practical value could such a question be?" The beauty which lies behind the repulsion is that these questions *are* of no practical value. Neither is being. Being stands of and for itself, with no qualifications or justifications. The only really important questions, then, are those which can't be answered. Just because we don't find an answer is no reason to stop asking. There's no need to turn our backs on these questions simply because they continually remind us of our stupidity.

How many angels? In college my friends and I used to sit up late in the night pondering these ultimate questions. It was a way of being comrades, almost like playing a game, doing something so we could be friends together. But it was more than that. We were serious about finding answers. We still thought it was possible. When we'd finally and drowsily make our way to bed, the questions would still be spinning in our minds. And in the morning, when the cigarette smoke and the sleepiness had cleared away, the questions would still be there.

During the day, in the middle of chemistry class, I'd catch myself thinking about the questions. And when I

should have been studying, I'd find myself writing about
them. What is the meaning of life? What is God? What is
the nature of truth? It was all very sophomoric, which was
appropriate because we were indeed sophomores. It seemed,
at the time, that with enough thinking and talking and
writing and living, we'd finally understand. We'd know. The
answers would come. It was a wonderful feeling. Sometimes
we'd feel so close. Close to the answers, and to each other.
And close to ourselves.

But eventually something happened. We weren't
sophomores anymore. And somehow it became more
important to learn how to get along in life than to learn why
we were alive. The answers weren't forthcoming, and I
suppose we were a little disappointed. So we each got busy
learning our trades, and the struggle for ultimate truth
drifted back somewhere into the realm of memories. Now
and then, in a moment of nostalgia, I would write again. And
on very rare occasions a friend and I might begin to talk
about the meaning of life. But it never was the same. A
certain spark had gone.

I don't think I ever quite got to the point of
scornfulness of these questions. But many of my friends did.
I guess unanswered questions make a person feel impotent.
So the questions themselves are attacked as meaningless.
Waste of time. I don't think any of us really wanted to give
up the search. But it seemed necessary. There was something
in it that demanded more than we were ready to give.
Besides, sitting around talking about the meaning of life was
not going to get us a good job or a new car or a secure sense
of identity. So most of us just went ahead with what was
socially and academically "appropriate" and kept a little
tender nagging sense that we'd been close to the truth and
then turned away from it. Others of us adopted a sour-
grapes rationalization. "Oh yeah, I used to think about all
that stuff. But that's just childish. It doesn't get you
anywhere. Like counting the angels on the head of a pin."

Some of the people who said this are very happy with
their lives now. Others are beginning to have a few more
drinks when they come home from work.

What very few of us understood was that none of the
things like security, job, even family would *mean* much
without our returning to the ultimate questions. And we
didn't realize that hanging out with the questions, letting
them come fully into our awareness, was much more
important than getting answers. We gave up because there
were no answers. But we gave up in the wrong direction. We
should have given up *into* the questions rather than turning
our backs on them. One thing that's nice, however, is that
it's never too late.

If there is a problem with meditation, shall we try to fix it? Certainly. But the fixing will be dangerous. Because problems are only defined by our very limited and arbitrary sense of what we like and what we don't like. What we want and what we don't want. Who knows, ultimately, what is a problem and what isn't?

Unfixing   It should be kept in mind that the more we fix our problems the more likely it is that we shall try to fix ourselves. And the more we try to make meditation work efficiently, the more we shall be using it to achieve something. On the other hand, the more we can accept, the more we can relax and be open to what is. The way through all of this is to do no *extra* fixing and to participate in no extra *avoidance* of fixing. However you find yourself in any moment, accepting or fixing, peaceful or struggling, *that* is what must be accepted. The totality of it.

Problems	Suggestions
1. I get sleepy when I meditate.	Look to your posture. Is it alert as well as relaxed? Sit up straight. Or go outdoors, or near an open window. Or breathe deeply and quickly for a while. Or try letting yourself go to sleep in the middle of meditation. Surround your little nap with awareness.
2. My knees hurt, my back hurts, I'm uncomfortable and I've got itches all over.	See how much you have to struggle with the discomfort. Can you accept it? If you can, let it be. If you must struggle with it, go ahead and move and scratch. Or use the discomfort as a base for attention. Go right into it and be there with it very intimately. But whatever, stay aware. Don't try to block it out. Don't go into a trance with it.
3. I feel irritable, depressed after meditation.	You're probably trying too hard. Probably want something you're not getting. Once you sit down to meditate, quit trying. Just relax and go with whatever's there. And make your transition *very slowly* at the end of meditation.

4. I feel "spaced out," sort of in a daze after meditation. Sometimes it's difficult to come "out" of meditation.

You're going "off" somewhere. Stay clear and bright here and now all through meditation. Pay attention to something here and now. Stay aware of the sights and sounds around you during meditation.

5. My mind is too noisy, no quietness happens.

Listen to the noise.

6. Meditation is boring.

It really is a blessing when all the color and excitement leaves meditation. But it may not feel like a blessing. Try seeing the boredom as emptiness. Let it be and go into it fully. Or watch yourself being bored. Explore the quality of the feeling.

7. I keep getting these same thoughts, dumb thoughts, going around and around in my head.

Try encouraging these thoughts. Go ahead and think them actively. Think Think Think. Use them for your base.

8. Anxiety. Agitation. Restlessness. "I just can't sit still any longer."

Try sensing the feeling of the anxiety. What is the quality of it? The color? The shape? Explore it face to face. Not get rid of it, but to see it clearly. If this is impossible, stop meditation and do something else. Shorten your meditation time and pay more attention to informal meditation.

9. My breathing scares me— it seems like I'm going to stop breathing and die. Or I get to breathing too fast.

This is a fear of losing control. Having experienced breathing without control, sometimes there's a backlash. Trying to get back in control for fear it won't be all right without you at the steering wheel. What to do? Relax again. Allow your fear and your need to control. Control what you feel you must. It will pass. And you *won't* stop breathing for too long.

10. I have very strange visions or body sensations or thoughts which scare me.

Again, it probably is your threatened self-image trying to defend itself. Back off when it gets too scary. Don't feel you must press on through. Allow the layers of control to peel off gently. Stop for a while if you need to. Just don't take it too seriously. Don't do any hard-pushing of yourself unless you have competent guidance.

11. I have very interesting, exciting, dramatic, supernatural experiences.

Same thing. Don't take it too seriously. Neither cling nor push.

12. After meditation, things seem unusually bright and colorful, and there's a lot of energy.

Fine.

13. I become very controlling and picky after meditation.

Again, it's the backlash of a threatened ego. You're probably trying too hard to give up. Ease off and let yourself be.

14. I'm encountering things in myself which I don't like at all.

It's to be expected. Accept the good and the bad of yourself. Don't get lost in trying to fix yourself up. Just do what seems right and best, and have some patience with who you are.

15. I feel I'm withdrawing from my family and friends as a result of meditation.

Maybe it's just the natural result of becoming more accepting of yourself so you don't need so much affirmation from others. Or it could be you're escaping into meditation. If you find meditation very enjoyable, try meditating a little less for a while.

16. I find meditation very helpful in coping with the stresses of daily life, and I'm using it more and more in this way.

Quit meditating for a while.

17. I keep finding exuses not to meditate. And yet when I do meditate, it seems good. I struggle with this.

Don't make such a big deal of it. It's probably your self-image trying to keep noisy. But you 'don't need to do battle. Set a reasonable schedule and follow it to a sensible degree. No extreme discipline. No extreme laziness. Walk a gentle middle ground.

18. I feel I really need a guide or a teacher.

You probably do. Sometimes it's really necessary. Just don't become frantic or fanatic about your master. He or she will be just another person, there for you to be with. You have many teachers. Friends, relatives, and enlightened masters. Approach them all with good common sense.

19. I feel very alone in my search.

So does most everyone. Try sharing your concerns with a few other people. Gently. You will probably be as relieved as they are to find out how much you share. Don't try to go it alone. But watch out that you don't wind up forming an exclusive group. As soon as you all start agreeing on basic philosophy, you've got a cult cooking.

20. Meditation is becoming a very important part of my life. A precious time, and I don't want anything to interfere with it.

What is the difference between meditation and the rest of life? Look more to informal meditation and ease off the heavy significance of formal meditation. Or quit it altogether. *Nothing* is *that* important.

21. No matter what I do, I can't get comfortable with meditation. It never seems right to me somehow. I feel like a failure as far as meditation is concerned.

Most likely you've been trying to meditate when you don't have any need to. Look closely at the rest of your life. Perhaps you've been meditating all along in other ways and just didn't realize it. And maybe you're trying to meditate formally because

for some reason you thought
you *should*. If so, formal
meditation will feel deeply
contrived and artificial. Not
right deep down inside you.
As well it should. Quit trying
to be something different
from who you are. Be, as you
are, and as you are becoming.

This section is meant to fulfill two purposes. First, it provides some suggestions for further readings in the heritage of open meditation. Second, it explores the nature of that heritage. This exploration will help the reader understand some of the historical influences which have had impact upon the approaches described in this book. But more importantly, it is a way for me to recognize my indebtedness to the community of pilgrims who have gone before and who now continue to serve, inspire and support my own search. It is a way of acknowledging my heritage.

It is perhaps a necessary evil that many people in our modern society begin their spiritual struggles in a random, superficial way, without any sense of heritage whatsoever. Experiencing this technique and that idea, this teaching and that understanding from the great metaphysical cafeteria, one faces the danger of tasting only the surface manifestations of things. Sooner or later, however, one can hope to realize that no matter how chaotic his or her approach may have seemed, there are very deep roots which feed it. Then perhaps one can begin to discover those roots, with wonder and reverence. One is perhaps never as alone as one might think.

On the surface it may appear that the perspectives in *The Open Way* are very eclectic. And to be sure, material has been drawn from a wide variety of spiritual and scientific traditions; from ancient eastern thought through Christian mysticism to modern psychology. But underlying this apparent diversity is a constant thread which can be identified with closer examination. This thread, if it can be stated at all, says something like the following:

> There is within you, right now, as you are and as you are becoming, the capacity to be in harmony with Ultimate Truth. And that same capacity allows for natural, pure processes of growth, healing, compassion and wisdom. One need do nothing to achieve one-ness, union or relationship with God. All this is already given, offered in every single instant of life. The problem is simply one of seeing what is already there; cutting through and clearing away the confusion, complexity and distorted perceptions which cloud our vision of that-which-is. Sin, evil and suffering arise from our failure first to recognize this reality and second to trust it. This is the human condition, which at its core is a sacred, dynamic process. Realizing one's basic harmony with this process involves freedom, clarity of awareness and a decreasing sense of self-importance. How one goes about moving toward this realization, regardless of personal faith or belief, is a great paradox. One must find oneself, but in the process one must also lose oneself. It cannot privately, willfully be accomplished. Still, one must try. It cannot be personally achieved. Still there it is, always.